The Housesitter's Guide to the Galaxy

The Housesitter's Guide to the Galaxy

A Guide to Housesitting and Achieving Sustainable, Eco-friendly Travel

Jessica Holmes

Copyright © Jessica Holmes 2023

The right of Jessica Holmes to be identified as author of this book has been asserted in accordance with the Copyright, Designs and Patents Act 1988.

First published in 2023 by Arena Books

www.arenabooks.co.uk

All rights reserved. No part of this publication may be reproduced, stored in a retrieval system, or transmitted, in any form, or by any means (electronic, mechanical, photocopying, recording or otherwise) without the prior permission of the publisher.

Arena Books does not have any control over, or any responsibility for, any author or third-party websites referred to in this book.

Jessica Holmes
The Housesitter's Guide to the Galaxy

British Library cataloguing in Publication Data. A Catalogue record for this book is available from the British Library.

ISBN: 978-1-914390-17-3 (paperback)
ISBN: 978-1-914390-18-0 (ebook)

Thema: WTD; WTHC; WTL; WTHA; WTHW; VSZ; WBL; WTHE; WMQF; RNB

Cover design by Luisa Galstyan.

*For Derek who always encouraged fun and adventure,
and to all those seeking freedom*

You cannot swim for new horizons until you have courage to lose sight of the shore.

William Faulkner

Contents

INTRODUCTION 1
ABOUT ME 4
HOUSESITTING – "WHAT'S THAT WHEN IT'S AT HOME?" 9
HOUSESITTING AND GREEN TRAVEL 10

TYPES OF HOUSESIT 12
PAID HOUSESITTING 12
UNPAID HOUSESITTING 14
HOUSESITS AND PET CARE – DO THEY GO HAND IN HAND? 17

HOUSESITTING WEBSITES 19
JOINING FEES, ANNUAL SUBSCRIPTIONS AND SITTER COSTS 20
WEBSITES 20
OTHER COSTS TO CONSIDER 22
YOUR HOUSESITTING PROFILE 23

HOUSESITTING AGREEMENTS AND ETIQUETTE 27
HOUSESITTING DO'S AND DON'TS 29

MY FAVOURITE HOUSESITS SO FAR 36
CASTROP-RAUXEL, GERMANY 36
BLOCKLEY 37
FOREST OF DEAN 38
LITTLE WASHBOURNE 38
RURAL SOMERSET 39
RURAL RUTLAND 40

IS HOUSESITTING FOR EVERYONE? 41

- THE SOLO TRAVELLER 43
- GROUP TRAVEL 44
- TRAVELLING AS A FAMILY 44
- PEOPLE TRAVELLING WITH PETS 45
- DISABILITY 45
- HOUSESITTING SUITS ALL AGES 46
- WHAT PERSONALITY IS NEEDED FOR HOUSESITTING? 46

COMMON ISSUES WHILE HOUSESITTING 48

- GETTING POST 49
- VOTING 49
- VISAS 50
- PASSPORTS 50
- VACCINATIONS 50
- CAR OR VAN INSURANCE 51
- SELF-CARE AND HEALTH ISSUES 51
- OTHER ISSUES TO CONSIDER WHEN HOUSESITTING OVERSEAS ... 53

HOUSESITTING STORIES: HIGH STEAKS 55

GETTING AROUND 59

- CARS 60
- BUSSES AND COACHES 61
- WITH ALL THESE POSITIVES, WHAT COULD GO WRONG? 63
- TRAVEL STORIES: SOMEWHERE IN THE NETHERLANDS, JANUARY 2023 65
- FERRIES AND SHIPS AND OTHER WATER TRANSPORT 71
- CYCLING 72
- MOTORBIKES / SCOOTERS 73
- TRAINS 75
- CAMPERVANS / MOTORHOMES 78
- ON FOOT 79
- HITCHHIKING 81
- TRAVEL STORIES: A BRUSH WITH THE LAW 83
- AIR TRAVEL 84

LIFE ON THE ROAD 87

- TRAVEL LIGHT 87
- HOUSESIT GEAR ESSENTIALS 89

STAYING ECO-FRIENDLY ON THE ROAD 93
PACKING HACKS 95

HOUSESITTING STORIES: ALL'S WOOL THAT ENDS WOOL 100

IN-BETWEEN HOUSESITS 103

PAID ACCOMMODATION 103
COUCHSURFING 105
VOLUNTEERING 106

VOLUNTEERING ON THE ROAD 107

WWOOFING 108
WORKAWAY 109
HELPX 110
VOLUNTOURISM 111

ECO-TOURISM AND ECO-TRAVEL 113

HOW DO I FIND ECOTOURIST PROJECTS? 115
ECO ACCREDITATIONS AND CERTIFICATES 117
SOME EXAMPLES OF ECO-TOURIST DESTINATIONS AND PROJECTS
.... 119
HOW HOUSESITTING FITS IN WITH ECO-TOURISM 121

SLOW AND SUSTAINABLE TRAVEL 122

SUSTAINABLE TRAVEL 125
WHERE TO GO (AND WHERE TO AVOID) AS A SUSTAINABLE
TRAVELLER 126
STAYCATION 126
OVER TOURISM – PLACES TO AVOID 126
WHEN TO TRAVEL 128
UNDER-TOURISM 130
DISASTER TOURISM 130
HOW HOUSESITTING FITS IN WITH SLOW AND SUSTAINABLE
TRAVEL 131
TRAVEL STORIES: THE CHERRY ON TOP 134

RESPONSIBLE TRAVEL 136

BEING CULTURALLY SENSITIVE 136

HOW TO BE GREEN IN SOMEONE ELSE'S HOME 140

DIGITAL NOMADS, HOMEWORKERS AND HOUSESITTING 151
HOUSESITTING STORIES: OUR BIG SHOT 156
THE THERAPEUTIC BENEFITS OF HOUSESITTING .. 159
A NOTE FOR THE HOMEOWNER 167
Housesitting from the homeowner's perspective: 168
FREEDOM 174
THE TOP 10 BENEFITS OF HOUSESITTING 176
FAQS 181
THE NOMADIC DICTIONARY 186
USEFUL WEBSITES 192
Housesitting websites 192
Paid housesitting websites 193
Pet first aid 194
Travel volunteering & connecting 194
Carbon calculators / offsetting schemes 195
Outdoor recycled gear 196
Green travel choices 197
Green travel accreditations 199
Modes of transport 201
Other useful stuff 202
BIBLIOGRAPHY 204
AUTHOR BIO 211

Introduction

If you think adventure is dangerous, try routine, it is lethal.
Paulo Coelho

I'm keeping my footsteps as light as I can on the yellow, brown and red leaves layering the grassy field, and listening hard to the sounds of wildlife that envelope me. A choir of chaffinches twitter away as they swoop past me at shoulder height, a wood pigeon makes its distinctive call nearby, two robin tenors sing animatedly to one another on a fence and the screeching hoot of a barn owl emerges from a derelict outbuilding in the adjoining field. A squirrel catches my eye a few metres away and I stop and bend down to hear the leaves rustling in the breeze. Touching the ground with my hands I note that this sacred ground is home to so much diverse wildlife. Vivid images flash through my mind – of voles and dormice tunnelling through grass, badgers dozing cocooned inside setts, and foxes dashing across open ground. But today, I have come here to witness a different mammal altogether.

The sunrise is just above the horizon and amber gold hues are tumbling through the wooded area to the right of the field, casting long shadows that silhouette the outlines of tall trees and the remaining leaves left on their lofty branches. The crunch of a frosty leaf underfoot betrays my presence and I freeze as at least fifty pairs of eyes look in my direction. Majestic and enigmatic, the herd move their heads as one. Their coats appear auburn in the morning light and distinctive white spots cover their backs. The fallow deer are an elegant breed, preferring deciduous woodland with large clearings. I can see their breath as it expels and hits the cold air. As they continue to stare at me, assessing whether I pose any threat to them, I know I've got as close to them as I should. Maintaining complete stillness, I take in their beauty and soak up the tangible aura of magic they invoke in me. Seeing any animal in their natural habitat always fills me with joy. Once I've taken a few minutes to revel in this one-on-one time with the herd, I turn back. It's a mere two-minute walk back to the snug cottage and cuddly cat I'm looking after, and I've left a cafetiere of locally ground coffee brewing ready for my return.

***

Are you a lover of travel who is painfully aware of your own carbon footprint? Does this result in you being plagued by moral dilemmas every time you start to plan a trip? What if I told you that I'd found the secret to long-term sustainable and environmentally friendly travel? What if I also told you that it is pretty much free to live in this way, and that actually you could save money whilst enjoying this lifestyle? "Nah, she's gone mad", I hear you scoffing.

Cosy cottages, beachfront bungalows, clifftop cabins, rural ranches, chateaus, townhouses, suburban, isolated, city-centre, lakeside, Europe, Africa, America; whatever and wherever you fancy, there's a housesit out there for you. If you grab the opportunity that housesitting presents, you could soon be going on holiday or travelling full-time while saving money and travelling responsibly at the same time.

Housesitting is a phenomenon which has grown in popularity in the UK and worldwide over the last decade; it is the ingeniously simple concept of living in and looking after other people's

Introduction

homes whilst they are temporarily away. With websites and apps set up specifically to facilitate the process of finding a house to look after, or a person to look after your house, the practice has never been more prevalent and widespread than now, when mobile phones or laptops are usually no more than arms reach away from most of us.

My husband and I are nomadic people who love to live life on the road. Last year, in 2022, we began to travel using housesits as an enabler and solution to maintaining long-term travel for us both. Now, a few months into our housesitting-cum-travelling journey, and enjoying every day of our simpler, slower lifestyle, I have decided that it's time to spread the word. I've been speaking to local people in the places we are staying, and have realised that although this is a concept that is becoming more known and accepted worldwide, there is still a shockingly low number of people using housesitting as a means of facilitating their travels, and homeowners as means of having their homes and pets looked after. Every time I tell people that we travel full time using housesitting for accommodation and that we are so committed to the process that we rented out our house in the UK, people are amazed and shocked, and usually very interested in how they can do something similar.

In the current global state of post-pandemic economic crisis, skyrocketing rents and household bills, and increasing environmental damage and biodiversity loss, it has never been more critical to be aware of the impact that travel and tourism is having on the environment; and to find a way to travel that is more environmentally and financially ethical.

The *Housesitters Guide to the Galaxy* is your go-to guide for information on what housesitting is, the best way to use housesitting to facilitate your short-term holidays or new nomadic lifestyle, and for finding out how you can achieve slow, sustainable, responsible and eco-friendly travel.

About me

I grew up a nature lover, and always curious and questioning, I became a young woman who wanted to see the world. I'm not sure whether it was my love of reading about far-flung places or the imagination of my geography teachers that fuelled the intrinsic need to travel. I also had a great love of animals and conservation which ignited my desire to want to help protect wildlife and combat environmental issues worldwide. I didn't go on family summer holidays every year or have a wise grandparent regaling me with tales of distant lands, but I knew that my future was "out there".

Regardless of this knowledge, I did what every good student does and stuck at school, got good A Levels (including Food Technology; which a professor at Cardiff University told me "wasn't a real subject" – needless to say I didn't apply to go there, what a pompous git) and went to Swansea University, Cardiff's main rival – take that, Sir! I wasn't sure what I wanted to do at university and felt a bit pressured into making a decision; it ended up being Criminology; the study of crime and criminals. I forgot to tell you, I also have what some may call an unhealthy obsession with crime fiction, murder mysteries and anything Agatha Christie.

I went to university, got a first-class degree which people wondered if I would do anything with and low and behold I didn't (initially). In my third year of university I started a relationship with a boy who had a passion for everything travel and anything me; needless to say we are now married. This wonderful human gave me the confidence and security to realise my dream. I wanted to travel, far and wide, as long term as possible, and definitely with him. Off we went for two years round the world, visiting non-conventional travel hubs such as Russia and Mongolia, before hitting the Asian backpacker trail and ending up in Australasia for a year and a half. We came home, excited to see family and friends and full of tales to tell, we were still in our early twenties and young and naïve. It was

Introduction

expected then – by our family, our friends, or wider society perhaps – that we would settle down. So that's what we did; we bought our first home and got "proper" jobs. I joined the police and Tom qualified to become an accountant. I decided to work my way into investigations and then towards the Major Crime team, where I could investigate sudden deaths and murders and where I knew I would thrive.

Over the four years we were settled in one place, we never lost our sense of adventure and longing for travel and planned a big, pull-out-all-the-stops trip to South Africa. We wanted culture shock. I wanted to go on safaris and see animals I'd only dreamed of. We wanted experiences and we needed to get out of the UK, like now. This meticulously planned trip of a lifetime was kiboshed by the pandemic, it died a death, and that was when we realised we needed to act. We were travelling people, nomads, adventurers, explorers, discoverers, not corporate employees cooking casseroles and doing the washing. Routine had killed our dreams. Societal expectations and norms had forced us to conform. But no more! The pandemic pushed us to really knowing who we were. We loved our jobs and our home, but they were essentially trapping us and pinning us down to being in one location, making us "stay put". We knew that the conventional lifestyle was not for us; life isn't a "one size fits all" affair. When the pandemic put paid to our hopes and dreams of African adventures and any other trips abroad, we went a bit stir crazy. We worked out that it was the longest period that either of us hadn't been abroad since we were in our teens. We set about finding a way that we could travel indefinitely. And then as soon as we could walk, we would run.

Although I was flourishing within the Major Crime team, and my husband Tom was enjoying his job in accountancy, we both felt a nagging that we weren't on the right path. Tom started looking for a job that he could do remotely from anywhere. And I had the desire to write but could never find the time or energy when I was employed full time – and financially I couldn't afford to quit my job. When Tom secured a fully remote role in the summer of 2022, I knew we should act soon. We had done a few housesits after being introduced to the concept by a family in China in 2016. They had been on the road for a few months with their eight-year-old child and had been home schooling her. I found out recently that they're still on the road now – very impressive. We started doing local housesits while still working full time and living at home; we'd spend our free weekends doing them, building up reviews on our profile and enjoying a free weekend away in the UK.

A few months later, we had a chat in our garden. I can't remember which of us initiated the conversation but it turned out that both of us had been thinking the same thing. What was to stop us doing housesitting full time? We discussed this brainwave at length, like children huddled in a corner planning to run away from home, it was all we talked of, thought of and dreamt of.

Of course, it was a massive thing for us to even think of leaving our home permanently; we'd spent a few years painstakingly cultivating our garden and decorating the interior of the house. We felt secure and protected by the bricks and mortar that made up our home. It's no small feat to consider stepping outside of the comfort zone that a home provides you. It's not something to be rushed into or done without seriously considering all the positives and negatives.

For me, the hardest and most difficult decision to make was the fact that I'd have to quit my job for us to embark on a full-time housesitting lifestyle; investigating murder simply isn't something that can be done remotely. I'd worked since my late teens towards being in the police, and since I'd joined the constabulary I'd then worked my arse off to get into Major Crime, where I'd only been working for six months. I'd recently completed something called Professionalism in Policing (PIP) Level 1 which comprised of six months of studying for an exam which I'd bossed with a high pass. It had also meant spending fifty hours writing evidence into a portfolio to show that I could

Introduction

investigate crime, recover and retain evidence, and interview witnesses and suspects in custody. None of this work was easy, and all of it was done alongside my full-time job in the police. I'd been the best I could be in the police and proven to myself and others that I really did belong in investigations. Not only that – but I'd gotten into the Major Crime team, no easy thing for a young woman with only a few years of experience behind me. The Detective Chief Inspector that interviewed me said I'd gotten the best interview scores that he'd seen for a long time. I was proud of my achievements in the police, and I was more than proud of my career. I loved my job. You can imagine the laughs that it got when I turned up to crime scenes and officers took note of my credentials, "Holmes, is it? ... Really?", they'd say, one Avon and Somerset officer declared, "Sherlock's here", when I arrived at the scene of a sudden death. Everyone would crack a smile or laugh, and I'd laugh along with them – maybe it was fate that when I married Tom I became a Holmes.

But I was living as two different people. Cheating on my job by day-dreaming about fulltime travel. Cheating on travel by continuing to be a career-driven woman. Neither could be the priority for me while I still romanced the idea of the other. Like Harry Potter and Voldemort; neither could live while the other survived. I was quickly speeding towards a crisis point, two intersecting life lines crossing over, and a big decision needed to be made.

I was doing this soul searching during the summer of 2022, and remembered a book I'd read a few years previously – the Chimp Paradox. A book I'm sure a lot of you have read or at least heard of. There's a section within Steve Peters' book in which he describes what he calls the "Stone of Life" – a list of three things that make up a person's perspective on life, or their life reference point (Peters, 82-86). The "Stone of Life" is made up of a person's "Truths of Life", their "Values" and their "Life Force". The one that came flooding back to me while I sat in this quandary was the latter. The "Life Force" is essentially what you believe life is about and how it should be lived. Peters says that you should imagine that you are elderly and on your death bed. A loved one asks you, "What should I do with my life?". How would you answer? Your answer shows what life is all about to you. Without any pausing, my answer to this question was, and still is, simply, "Travel." I had my answer. I quit my job the following week.

The next month was hectic. We had decided to rent out our house for a year initially and so we needed to find tenants. We also wanted to sell most of our furniture and household goods that we weren't precious about – we'd gotten most of our stuff from charity shops or second hand. There were only a few things in the house that we wanted to keep and these things we put into our attic and locked up. We found some tenants within a few weeks, and as luck would have it they wanted to buy some of our furniture – perfect! We were going to keep our car (we only shared one vehicle anyway as we had never needed two) as we would be using it to travel to our first few housesits within the UK. We wouldn't need much stuff so we began sorting through the piles of clothes and possessions that we had amassed during the last four years. Most went to charity shops, some went into storage in our attic, and before we knew it, we were ready to go.

We began moving from sit to sit at our leisure; we booked longer sits into our calendar, trying to get housesits for a minimum of one month if we could. This would give us time to settle into areas and actually unpack before we had to leave again. This lifestyle change meant that we would have a significant reduction in our bills as someone else would effectively be paying our mortgage, and we wouldn't have any household utility bills to pay. It was time for me to start writing; I took a leap of faith and started a blog as well as a social media account. I wanted to write small guides to the places we were visiting as well as a book. I was nervous and unsure but I found that writing came fairly easily to me. I did a few writing courses and began finding my own way around common problems such as writers block, generating fresh ideas, and motivation.

Introduction

And that brings us to today, where I am writing, and Tom is working next to me, and we are looking after someone's gorgeous home and even more gorgeous dogs. We are finally doing it; long-term sustainable travel that works for us, and I'm writing this book to tell you how it could work for you too.

Housesitting – "What's that when it's at home?"

Housesitting has long been a concept used to find trustworthy individuals to live in and look after people's homes - and often their pets too - whilst they are away. Traditionally, it has been a paid profession in which people are employed to look after large, unoccupied houses or estates for wealthy owners concerned about the risk of burglary. More recently however, housesitting has developed into a phenomenon that is accessible to everyone, meaning anyone can have their home looked after, and anyone can become a "housesitter". It has grown in popularity all over the world and become a reputable way of combatting the issues of unoccupied houses and pet care combined.

The basics:

- You live in someone else's home while they are away
- You look after the home and keep it clean, tidy and well-kept
- You look after any pets that live there
- You use the homeowner's gas, electricity, water, broadband, Wi-Fi and other utilities, often their TV subscriptions and sometimes get insured on their vehicles too – but you don't pay any bills
- You can explore the surrounding areas at your leisure
- You get to travel the world in a slower more considerate way

You can choose to undertake housesitting occasionally, on a short-term basis, or you can make a permanent change in the way you live by making it a long-term commitment. If you choose the latter, not only are you leaving the space you feel safest in – the secure sanctuary that you've lovingly put together with just the right amount of scatter cushions from Homesense – but you're also packing away or selling most of your possessions (you definitely don't need to carry your own crockery or kitchen utensils with you!). It's definitely one hell of a change getting used to a new home; it always takes some adjustment but once you get past the initial few days in someone else's space you will eventually start remembering which cupboards things are kept in. After a couple of weeks, you will inevitably start forming personal opinions on the layout of the house such as "I would have put the cutlery in that draw," or "The pots and pans fit better in this cupboard," or even "The sofa would be better in the other corner of the room" – and that's when you know you're a couple of days away from being right at home in someone else's space. Our optimum sit-length is probably a couple of months, but we have a usual minimum of one month. Any less than that just feels hectic and uncomfortable for us seeing as we do this gig full time and have our entire lives stowed away in our car (note to any thieves out there; it's not actually in our car, we lug it into each house with us).

Housesitting and Green Travel

I wouldn't be writing this book unless there was a desperate need for us to begin considering our impact on the planet and on the natural environment. As a human race, we have always travelled; it is part of our nature, part of the way we connect with each other and educate ourselves. We will never stop completely. So, we need to make conscious decisions about how and when we travel to reduce pollution and our individual carbon footprints. Through our actions and decisions, we can influence policy makers in governments, the travel industry and our own friends, families, and communities to make positives steps towards a greener future.

Introduction

Housesitters Guide to the Galaxy is set up as a guide to encourage better travel practices and to promote conscious decision-making at all stages of the travel process: when planning your trip; when you're on the move; and when you're staying at your destination. This book will also hopefully help you to implement a greener lifestyle within your home, wherever you reside. Green travel is for life, not just for holidays.

Types of Housesit

All you've got to do is decide to go and the hardest part is over.
Tony Wheeler

Paid housesitting

Paid housesitting is exactly what it sounds like. You are usually employed by a company who promote their housesitting services via websites, national and local magazines and advertisements. Many owners of large estates, country residences and rural homes will look to employ a house-sitter through this route, and will pay a hefty sum for the privilege of ensuring their homes are occupied year-round. Due to the type of home they own, combined with irreplaceable priceless antiques and belongings it may be furnished with, they may feel that a paid sitter will be more dependable.

As the house-sitter, you would be a professional in this industry with references that support your experience, reliability and trustworthiness as a live-in home and pet carer. Certain people looking for house sitters may also prefer you to have experience in security, military or policing backgrounds and may pay more money for sitters with these qualities.

The companies who provide sitters to look after their homes often have an insurance policy that covers damage, loss or injury sustained to the property or sitter whilst the sit is in progress.

Types of Housesit

The homeowners may feel that this insurance is desirable and necessary to cover risk whilst they are away, and paying for the service will assist in putting their minds at rest.

Positives:

- You are paid a sum of money for each housesit.
- This could be considered more of a "career".
- You get to sit larger houses in grander surroundings.
- This is possibly a more stable option. If an owner has paid a deposit or fee for you to sit, then they are unlikely to cancel, and if they do, the company you are employed with would may reimburse your costs for other accommodation. They may even be required to pay you some of the fee you would have earned.
- You get to travel the world by housesitting.

Negatives:

- Irregular income amounts per month.
- Larger housesits could be considered more difficult; more rooms to keep clean and tidy, more pets with possibly more complex needs, more security surveillance to conduct.
- There will be a higher level of expectation from the owners.
- There is more of a risk of burglary and so you could be putting yourself in harm's way.
- It's a job – it's therefore much more formal than unpaid housesitting.
- Less freedom to pick your next assignment if the company requires specific qualities for certain housesits.
- A transient lifestyle isn't for everyone and it's difficult unpacking and repacking for each housesit.

Having never undertaken paid housesitting, this is not a speciality area for me. However, a simple Google search for paid housesitting jobs reveals several companies with whom you can sign up. One of these is Luxury House Sitting, another is Care.com which is broader and offers jobs such as childcare, tutoring and senior care as well as house and pet sitting. Paid housesitting work may also be advertised on national sites such as Reed or Indeed, where you can apply by sending your CV to the agency who have posted the advert. Rover is a website that has grown in popularity and marries up pet and housesitters with homeowners. On this website, the housesitter has a profile that shows their experience, reviews and the nightly fee to look after peoples' pets.

Unpaid housesitting

Unpaid housesitting is again exactly what it says on the tin; you look after someone's home and pets but you are not paid to do so. This type of housesit works entirely on reviews; you can review someone whom has looked after your house and they can also review you. On most websites the reviews are split into categories such as cleanliness, reliability, pet-care and organisation whereby you are marked out of five, and then there is also a free-text space to enter feedback comments to provide context to the ratings provided.

This review-based housesitting has boomed in popularity over the last decade, with websites and apps facilitating the process, making it accessible to people all over the world. The housesits are wildly varied; a quick search on the app we use shows that there is currently a cat to look after in Nairobi, Kenya, two dogs who require care in Astana, Kazakhstan and a parrot who needs company in a chateau near Toulouse, France. The homes can be based on desert plains, in mountainous terrain, metres from the ocean, in energetic cities, or small, sleepy villages. Sits can be available from 1 night to 1 year (or longer), depending on the needs of the homeowner.

It is so important to do your research before you agree to undertake a housesit. As mentioned briefly before, pets may have specific or complex needs, they may be larger breeds that

Types of Housesit

require experienced handling or need medication given to them. The homes may be rural and require you to have a vehicle to access it. If the homes are isolated, you need to consider the length of the sit and the impact on your mental health. If you rely on remote work to keep you going while you housesit, you need to consider the Wi-Fi connection and speed at each location. As this type of housesit is unpaid, you will also be required to either live off savings or work whilst you sit. This can be a difficult balance to strike as some housesits come with a fair amount of tasks e.g. walking dogs, cleaning poultry runs, checking on livestock, mucking out stables – before you sign up, really consider whether you will be able to take on the necessary tasks alongside your other work and personal activities.

It can be quite difficult to secure your first few housesits on websites where the process is wholly review based. To tackle this issue, my husband and I decided that before taking the plunge and housesitting full time, we would build up our reviews by conducting short housesits close to our home. We would keep certain weekends free, about one per month, and search for housesits within our own county. We then worked on a "script" that we would use when reaching out to homeowners. If the sit had pets, we would keep the pets at the forefront of the application, stating our experience with stronger dogs, or our love of cats. We found that addressing the homeowners and pets by name made the message more personal. And stating our availability to talk on the phone, video call, or in person beforehand was a good way of building trust and securing a sit, and for housesits abroad we always arranged a video call.

Our commitment as house sitters doesn't stop once we've secured a sit; we keep in contact until the start date of the sit. And throughout the sit we update the owners with pictures of their pets and updates about what we've been doing. This is a fundamental part of providing a good service as a home and pet sitter. There is nothing worse than being away from your home and pets and worrying about how everything is going. We always conduct a deep clean before we leave a housesit; we clean and tidy all the areas of the house that we have used, wash our bedsheets and towels, and generally leave the house in a nice condition for the owners to come home to. We leave a thank you card and a small gift for them too. In a nutshell, if you want to secure housesits and good reviews – research, reach out, communicate, and clean!

Positives:
- You can conduct this type of travel alone, with your spouse, your family members, and sometimes even with your own pet (although this is rarer as most housesits have pets to look after as well) whereas paid housesitting is usually lone contractor work.
- It's less formal and more enjoyable than paid housesitting – it's not your job!
- You get to travel the world one housesit at a time.
- You have more freedom over where you travel; you apply to each housesit and can do this by looking at availability throughout the world.
- You are not paying for accommodation or most utility bills.
- You bond with homeowners and pets before and throughout the sitting process; you will often be asked back for future housesits at the same location.
- You can explore areas which you never would have booked a holiday in, or alternatively choose a housesit based on its location.

Negatives:
- You may need another source of income to sustain your livelihood.
- It's difficult to secure your first few sits if they are review based.

- Possibly more risky; the housesitters could cancel or simply not turn up, likewise the hosts could turn away a house sitter due to cancelled trips or other issues.
- A transient lifestyle isn't for everyone and it's difficult unpacking and repacking for each housesit.
- Some pets can be more difficult to look after than you envisaged.

Housesits and pet care – do they go hand in hand?

The unpaid housesitting that we conduct more often than not also has pet care thrown into the mix. On the app that we use, searching worldwide and unfiltered dates shows me that there are currently just 10 housesits available with no pets to look after. Getting pets looked after at kennels or professional boarders is currently very expensive. In the UK, prices for cat care average at approximately £12 per day (a 24% increase from 2019), and UK prices for dog care average at approximately £22 per day (a 22.5% increase from 2019). It's no wonder then that pet owners are looking for hassle-free solutions for times when they need to travel without their pets. Review-backed and free house sitters are an imaginative and effective way of combatting this global problem.

Some pets and housesits are more time consuming than others. For example, cats are usually very independent and if they have a cat flap it means that you can be out of the house for longer periods of time without worrying too much whether they are inside or outside. Animals that are caged within the home such as birds, rabbits and hamsters, usually only need feeding a couple of times a day, their water kept topped up, and some social interaction, to be well looked after. Other animals such as reptiles or fish in tanks may need feeding even less, and don't get removed from their tanks at all. This is obviously subjective and depends on the need of each animal; be sure to read all about them prior to applying for the housesit. The homeowner often prepares a "responsibilities" page which will have in-depth information about the specific needs of their pet. If you feel that you would prefer to look after pets with less "needs", then you can usually filter your searches for housesits by pet type, depending on the website you use.

On the other hand, if you're a lover of all animals – dogs, livestock, horses, the muddier the better, then you can remove all pet filters and look at everything available. On the housesitting site we use, the most common pets to look after are dogs and cats; this is probably because they are the most widespread domesticated animals and can live in most locations and house types.

The most important thing about pet-care is making sure that you aren't biting off more than you can chew. If you aren't experienced with stronger, larger breeds of dogs, don't say you are! If you really can't stand cats, don't apply for the housesit with five cats. You won't enjoy the housesit if you struggle to care for the pets, but most importantly the pets won't be happy, and you can bet that it will show in your reviews.

Housesitting Websites

Trust your intuition, it never lies. Oprah Winfrey

In the new and ever-expanding world of housesitting, looking for a housesitting website or agency can be a daunting task. Some housesitting organisations have separate websites for each country e.g. Mindahome Australia and Mindahome United Kingdom, but others are worldwide.

It is vitally important that prior to joining any website, you have a think about what you would most like to get from a housesit.

Are you looking to travel the world? Or do you want to use the site for holidays? Do you want to travel in one specific country? Do you only want to look after houses, not pets? Or do you definitely want to look after pets as well? Do you want a website which has an app version for you to use easily whilst on the road? Do you want 24/7 specialist support available via the website for any issues with the housesit? Is being able to use a map search view important to you? Do you want to be able to pay extra for additional support and insurance? Or do you want to sign up with minimal fees to begin with, ensuring that housesitting is right for you before you shell out?

Once you've thought about what you would like from housesitting, you can begin to compare the housesitting websites to find out which one is the right one for you. I would recommend that you don't rush this process, it's vital in ensuring you end up using the platform which will work best for you.

Joining fees, annual subscriptions and sitter costs

Most housesitting websites that are unpaid and review-based are subject to a joining fee and an annual subscription payment. These vary in cost and can be anywhere between £20-£200 depending on which site you go for and what level of subscription you want. There it is, the hidden cost. You might be saying, "so it's not as easy as she says," but hear me out. These fees are fairly low for the quality of service you will be provided with from each online housesitting platform. As a rule of thumb, usually the more expensive the platform is to join and maintain membership of, the higher quality service you will receive; system issue support, vet helplines, insurance and customer services are included in several of the more expensive sites. And what is £200 a year if you're not paying for accommodation? It's a very cheap investment in your new lifestyle and a small price to pay for the freedom that housesitting provides.

Websites

The leading and most popular housesitting websites are easy to find on the internet and are reviewed below. All of these websites require an annual fee for the facilitation of the housesitting process; hosting housesitter profiles, hosting homeowner profiles, and marrying the two to make the concept work. The websites also often provide supports such as those outlined above e.g. customer service and advice lines.

Below I have outlined the website subscription costs (correct as of October 2022) and the most prominent positives and negatives of each. Some of these points will be more important to you than others – for example, you may take comfort from a 24/7 support line and therefore be willing to pay more for it, or you may want specifically sits only within the UK and therefore may be more likely to go with a particular host platform. As with other parts of the housesitting process, all of these decisions are quite personal and individual.

Trusted Housesitters
£99 basic annual subscription for house sitters and homeowners (standard option available for £129 and premium for £199 – these options included additional extras such as home and contents protection, money back guarantees, video calls with vets whenever needed and even airport lounge passes)
+ Largest and most used housesitting website, worldwide sits available, for extra fee additional options for insurance over cancellations, free access to 24/7 member support and vet advice, user friendly website and app, verification process for all members, great review process.
- Most expensive option.

House Carers
£35 annual subscription for house sitters, free for homeowners
+ Reasonable fee, worldwide housesits available, email notification option
- Website not as user friendly as other housesitting website options.

Nomador
£80 annual subscription for house sitters, free for homeowners
+ Free trial option available to all, large range of housesits available, "stopover" feature is similar to couch surfing and a niche in the housesitting world
- This website is mainly limited to European housesits, rather than worldwide. And it's more pricey than other options.

House Sit Match
£80 annual subscription for house sitters, free for homeowners
+ ID checks included in fees, additional police check option available

- More pricey than other options, not as many housesits as other sites and locations less varied too.

Mindahome (different websites for UK and Australia)
£15 annual subscription for house sitters, free for homeowners
+ Email notification option, reasonable fee, reply rating of homeowners visible which helps sitters check communication standards
- Different membership for each country so less sits available, website not as user friendly as other options.

House Sitters (different websites for Australia, New Zealand, UK, America and Canada)
£30 annual subscription for the UK site, £55 for the other versions, free for homeowners
+ User friendly websites, reasonable fee, email notification option, layout of website makes it clear and easy to use
- Different membership for each country so less sits available, less sits available in general compared to other sites.

Mind My House
£20 annual subscription for house sitters, free for homeowners
+ Worldwide housesits available
- Can be competitive, often more sitters than houses available which could be a problem for sitters.

Other costs to consider

As well as annual subscription costs, there are also some costs of living which you need to factor into your housesitting lifestyle. These may sound obvious, but it is important to think about them if you are going to budget efficiently (can you tell I married an accountant?).

These costs include but are not limited to:

- Food for you and anyone else at the sit
- Travel costs to and from each housesit, use of public transport whilst there

- Vehicle associated costs such as petrol, insurance, tax, MOT, finance and cleaning
- Any additional utilities you may wish to purchase e.g. sky sports, now TV or more niche apps which the homeowner may not have a subscription to
- Eating and drinking out
- Beauty or health regimes e.g. gym, fitness classes, massages, nail extensions, haircuts
- Any bills you pay monthly e.g. phone bill, travel insurance, home insurance, life insurance, website or blog fees
- Entry fees for visits to nearby national parks and points of interest
- Any other activities you may wish to undertake in the area

Your housesitting profile

Writing your profile for a housesitting website is a bit like writing your profile for a dating website; you need to introduce yourself, some of your qualities, and what you are looking for. However, instead of "Female, late 20's, nature-lover and cat-cuddling enthusiast seeks nature loving, cat-cuddle-tolerating male whom does the washing up" (yep, I've found him), you need to sell yourself along with all of your relevant experience and qualities to the people you are asking to trust you with their most valuable belongings; their home and their pets. You want your whole profile to sound upbeat, enthusiastic and professional. If you have specific needs or requirements from a housesit, you should make it clear in your profile. This is your chance to really get your personality across to the people whose homes and pets you will soon be caring for; make it count.

First of all, you need to introduce yourselves, what's your name, where do you come from, what are your hobbies and interests; all of the usual gumpf goes in this section.

Most importantly, you now need to cover your experience of looking after people's homes and/or pets. This could be as simple of having looked after a friend's goldfish whilst they were away to living in and looking after people's homes and pets on numerous occasions. If you think it's relevant, put it in. Experience of looking after different types of homes is important here – whether that's gated mansions or tenth-floor flats, which countries you've looked after homes in, and whether you're content with being rural or would prefer city life. Showing your awareness of different household responsibilities is also key in this section, for example, if you're a keen gardener you could add in that you are happy to maintain garden areas, greenhouses and plants etc. Adding something in as basic as the fact that you will water any indoor plants during your stay will show homeowners that you understand the full breadth of responsibilities that come with housesitting.

It's crucial to put your experience with different types of animals in this section too. For example, let potential hosts know if you are strong and confident walking larger dogs, or if you've herded sheep, cuddled ferrets, or nursed a sick chicken back to health (yes we've done all of these things). Are you an animal lover? If you are, really lean into this. People's pets are like family members to them and they want the best people looking after their pets. Be enthusiastic in your writing about animals to make sure your eagerness to look after their pets really shines through.

If you feel it's of relevance, or if you particularly want people to know what you do, then add your occupation to your profile. What I mean by "relevance" here is does, for example, your occupation (or previous occupation/s) show a particular level of responsibility, skill or expertise? If you've worked for any company involving animals, such as dog-walking, pet grooming or in a veterinarian's, then make this stand out on your profile. If you have worked for a security company, or have previous policing or military backgrounds, mention this and explain how the skills you have built up will enhance the level of care you can give to host's home and pets. These are just a few examples; there will be many occupations and skillsets out there which inspire more thorough confidence in house sitters.

Qualifications that you have attained and feel are applicable to house and pet-sitting should also be added to your profile. For example, ask yourself: Do you have a pet first aid course? Do you have a pet first aid kit? Are you a horse rider or member of the British Horse Society? Do you have credentials for dealing with livestock? Have you done work experience with animals? You might in any case consider completing a pet first aid course; you can do this 100% online or in a mixture of online and in-person sessions from around £25.

There is usually a section on your profile to add photos. Trusted Housesitters allow you to add up to 10 images. Make your selection carefully; you want to get across some of your hobbies and interests, whether this be cycling, foraging or going to the pub! Another important tip that may sound obvious but is often overlooked, is to make sure that the photos show all those who will be doing the housesit; if you are a family, choose family photos, if you are a couple, choose photos with both of you – as well as the names of everyone in the group. The best type of photos to upload are those of you looking after other people's pets. If you can combine these three things you're on to a winner. So let's say you're a solo traveller who loves mountaineering; a photo of you, hiking with a dog you're caring for is what you're looking for. The more housesits you complete, the more great photos you'll have to upload.

Golden rule: Don't fabricate or embellish any part of your profile. Not only will people be choosing you based on certain qualities or qualifications you hold, but when you speak to people on the site and/or in person, they will ask you about things you have written and you do not want to be in a position where you cannot elaborate on topics or areas you have said you have an interest in.

Last but not least, be sure to keep your profile up to date. This is the part that is easy to forget about. When you start securing housesits, you know that your hard work has paid off and that your profile is of a good standard; you've hit the sweet spot and it's easy to think you needn't look at your profile again. However, maintenance is key! It may be something minor like a job change, a qualification expiring, your location changing (yes, I understand that's the point of travel), or something major like you were housesitting solo previously, but are now part of a housesitting couple. If an update to your profile is required, make the time to do it.

Housesitting Agreements and Etiquette

The real voyage of discovery consists not in seeking new landscapes, but in having new eyes. Marcel Proust

Most of the time, housesits go extremely well, with happy homeowners, house-sitters and pets at the end of the sit. We've not had a bad experience yet, but that's not to say others haven't. Having conducted some research on this topic it's clear that at least over 90% of housesits are satisfactory for all involved. The key to a successful housesit, for both you and the homeowner, is to be completely transparent in your expectations and for communication to be relevant, efficient and frequent. Most misunderstandings are the result of a mix-up in expectations. A lot of people find it difficult to be clear and firm in their requirements from the sit; this may be due to the fact that there is no payment involved by either party and that the contract being drawn up between you is more a contract of trust than a physical contract. However, outlining the requirements and expectations from the housesit in advance, is an important unspoken responsibility for both parties.

For homeowners, they want someone to look after their home and pets in the same way that they would. They want frequent updates from the house-sitter. Pictures of the pets are a great way of doing this because you don't want to message them so much that they can't enjoy their holiday. They want the house-sitter to arrive when agreed, and also to depart when agreed, leaving the house clean and tidy and the pets relaxed and happy. If they do have pets, they will want you to walk, cuddle and fuss their pets in the same way they do, sticking to their normal routine so as not to unsettle them further. They will also want the house sitter to be alert to any suspicious activity and to act as a security mechanism in the home.

On the other side of the agreement, the house-sitter will want clear instructions on the pet's routines. The instructions should be easy to follow and include information on the nearest vets, and feeding, cleaning and exercise routines. If the pets take medication or have any injuries, then their care routine needs to be clearly explained.

The location will have been discussed beforehand and will determine whether, for example, you need your own transport or not in a rural location, or if there is no parking in a city location. But once you arrive, the homeowner should communicate any quirks the house might have, such as a certain window not opening/closing, or a complicated heating system. If the house is big, they will need to be told the location of things such as clothes airers, vacuum cleaners and outside bins. The recycling and composting systems should be communicated, and the house-sitters left with the information on what day the different bins go out for collection. The homeowner also needs to specify whether the sitter needs to be aware of any tradesmen or visitors coming to the house during the sit.

House-sitters will be provided with a bed, bathroom, living space and kitchen facilities for the duration of their stay. The house should be generally clean and tidy on arrival for the house-sitters. If wi-fi is required by the house-sitters for remote working the homeowner should be open and honest about connectivity speeds. Homeowners should also specify if they have any external or internal CCTV and any other security devices such as alarms, ring door bells or any other voice monitoring equipment such as Alexa's and their locations around the home, as well as providing codes for any systems that need arming and disarming.

Most of this stuff is straightforward and discussed without the need for serious thinking, and if you do forget to ask where the vacuum cleaner is, contacting the owner to ask them once you've settled in isn't going to fill them with doubts that you can't do what you signed up to do. Likewise as a homeowner if you forget to mention something on handover or in any welcome guide you've left for the sitter, you can simply message them during their stay. Communication is the key to a successful trust exchange of this sort.

Housesitting Do's and Don'ts

I'm going to set the next section of this chapter out in "What not to do" based scenarios or examples for both parties; the homeowner and the house-sitter. A bit like the film "How to lose a guy in 10 days", a housesitting "how to" in reverse.

Don'ts for the Housesitter

- Agree to a housesit if you have no intention of looking after the house or the pets in the way that the owner has laid out
- Presume it's not your responsibility to clean, tidy and keep the house in good shape
- Move furniture around or rearrange cupboard items unless you have been told you can or you can put it back exactly how you found it. If you do need to move cupboard items to fit your own stuff in, take a picture of it before you move it so you can put it back in the right place.
- Invite guests round to visit or stay without express permission from the homeowner. In our experience this can be quite varied; some homeowners will say outright no to any visitors, others won't mind if they also stay overnight

whilst visiting. The most important thing here is communication.
- Leave pets unattended for long periods of time or have these conversations with the homeowner beforehand if you know you need to be out for a long time on some days. Most cats are quite independent and can be left longer but dogs all vary depending on their needs. The homeowner wouldn't have asked you to sit to leave their pets alone a lot of the time; they want them to have good quality company.
- Eat all their food. Most homeowners will tell you to eat any food in the fridge that's going to go off, some will leave you instructions of what you can't have e.g. expensive wine, and some will tell you to help yourself to anything. If you're not sure, don't eat it. A lot of homeowners will also leave you a gift on arrival such as a bottle of wine or chocolates. Don't take the mickey by leaving their cupboards bare for their return; if you do use something of theirs, replace it.
- Use their vehicles or equipment excessively. If the homeowner adds you to their car insurance, check the terms of use with them – do they mind if you use it daily or is it for exceptional circumstances? If they leave you bikes, scooters or a boat to use for recreational activity, check how much wear and tear it has when you initially use it, clean anything you use afterwards and if there is fuel in a vehicle before the sit, refill it to the same level when you leave.
- Mistreat pets in any way; this should go without saying, but mistreating can be a subjective word. Treat the pets the way the owner has told you to, and don't conduct any abusive or unfair behaviour towards the pets.
- Bring your own pets without asking – some homeowners will consider house-sitters with their own pet, but they will probably want the animals to meet before the sit takes place and check that they get on ok.
- Change the pets eating schedule, amount of food or type of food. Do not feed the pet any human food unless the owner has told you they sometimes have this. Any of these changes

Housesitting Agreements and Etiquette

could cause irritation for the pet and stomach illnesses such as pain, constipation or diarrhoea.

- Break things and hide them or not replace them. Best thing to do in this scenario is to tell the owner what you've broken. They can let you know if they want it replaced, or want some money towards a replacement, or if they aren't too bothered about it.
- Enter areas of the house which the homeowner has not allowed you access to; this could be a locked office or a whole wing of the house. Be respectful of the home you are staying in and understand that the owner may have important documents, expensive belongings or simply areas they want to keep private, or clean and tidy. The only exception to this is if there is an emergency such as a fire or if you are concerned there could be an intruder, or other similar serious issues.
- Arrive at the housesit late and leave early. Stick to agreed timings; there is nothing worse than the stress of getting the family together to go on holiday and worrying that a sitter may not show up at all. If arriving on time means arriving in the area the day before the housesit then do that. Don't leave early; the time agreed upon was probably due to the homeowners expected return time and the length of time the pets can be left alone. If you have an emergency that means you need to leave the property, explain this to the homeowner and come up with a solution together; you could take the pets with you, ask a neighbour to look after them for a day or use one of your emergency contacts as a suitable replacement.
- Cancel the housesit at the last minute. This is just not acceptable to do if you have a change of heart, receive a better offer or simply decide the sit is not for you. You must take the responsibility of house and pet sitting seriously and consider the financial, emotional and psychological impact of a cancellation on the homeowner. If you have an emergency or flight cancellation then you may be left with

no choice but to cancel the housesit as a last resort; try to find a suitable alternative to step in, or compensate the owners for any costs they may have to fork out for kennels or a paid sitter in your absence.

Don'ts for the Homeowner:

- Leave the house a complete mess, with the expectation that the house-sitter will clear it up when you've gone. Leaving for a holiday is stressful and busy, especially if you have children, but try to be considerate of the house-sitter.
- Leave dirty sheets and towels for the house-sitter to use; they should be clean and if possible the bed made up for the arrival of the sitter.
- Be vague about dates. Arrival and departure dates on the apps are sometimes guestimates by the homeowners of their holiday dates; they often want to secure a house-sitter prior to booking their holidays. This is understandable but needs to be communicated to the house-sitter and dates/timings clarified once the holiday is booked. The house-sitter may be coming to you from another sit, have booked annual leave for the duration of the sit or may have other commitments and appointments that could need rescheduling if your dates change. Be considerate and keep them in the loop.
- Expect the house-sitter to take care of unpaid utility bills unless previously discussed and agreed upon; the house-sitter should not be paying on your behalf or facing power, water or internet cuts due to outstanding payments to your providers.
- Add extra pets to the arrangement at the last minute. If you are going to have another pet by the time the housesit starts, let the sitter know! If you were going to get one more challenging pet looked after by someone else and they cancel on you, check that the sitter is ok to look after them and if not, find an alternative solution – don't force the sitter to

Housesitting Agreements and Etiquette

accept the additional pet without being open and honest about their specific needs.

- Cover up or play down any behavioural issues your pet may have. "Well behaved" is subjective and the sitter will be surprised if your pet is actually quite needy or naughty when you haven't made it clear. Specify to the sitter any particular things they do which they need to watch out for – do they chew shoes? Do they try to jump up a lot? Do they need a lot of attention? Alongside this, you need to make clear to house-sitters any additional characteristics or behaviours the pets have that may not be considered "run of the mill" to house-sitters. If they aren't toilet trained, continually bark or have aggressive traits you need to make it very clear; you will still find a house-sitter, and the contract of trust will work more smoothly as you have been honest. Do not request irrational pet care such as telling the sitter the pet cannot ever be left alone, or that they must sleep in the bed with them, or they have to be let outside 5 times a night.

- Expect the house-sitter to live in conditions which you wouldn't live in yourself. For example, telling them they can't turn the heating on in winter, or that they're not allowed to open the windows on a boiling hot day (unless there is genuine risk of pet escape issues such as indoor cats). Taking the control of the heating, lighting and water away from the house-sitter is quite demeaning and condescending. In this day and age, many homeowners have access to these systems on their phones. If the contract of trust is going to work, you need to trust them. If you are worried about the expense of the energy bills while you are away, discuss this with the sitter and ask them to only put it on when absolutely necessary. Make sure that the sitter has access to enough of the property to be comfortable during their stay; they need a comfortable living space, bedroom, bathroom and kitchen as a minimum (these can be family bathrooms and the main kitchen).

- Leave your child at home. House-sitters are not babysitters or childminders and if they haven't agreed to a teenager roaming around the house, don't leave them there. Likewise, don't expect the house-sitter to host your family or friends coming to stay in the house. This could cause unnecessary confusion for your pets, additional tasks for the house-sitters such as cleaning additional rooms and if not agreed upon, could leave the house-sitter feeling unsure of their responsibilities. Trusted Housesitters have a code of conduct for homeowners and house-sitters and one of the points stipulated is "I will ensure my home is vacated for my sitter throughout the duration of the sit, with no third parties present other than my confirmed sitter."
- Move house without telling the sitter, in the time between the housesit being confirmed and the housesit taking place. If you have agreed they will be staying in your home and you have provided them with information about the area, perhaps giving them a town or city name or address, but you know that by the time the sit takes place you could be living in another location – tell the sitter. Being open and honest on this point is really important. We've had housesits before where the homeowners have put a larger city or town nearby as their "location" and then when we arrive or they send us the address it is actually somewhere else, perhaps without public transport or similar amenities. This is an unfair thing to do to a housesitter as they may be applying to the sit based on its location.
- Cancel the housesit last minute. I understand this is sometimes unavoidable in cases of emergency or holiday cancellations, but make sure you understand the financial, emotional and psychological impact of you cancelling the sitter; they may have nowhere else to go and may have to stay in a hotel or Airbnb for the duration of the sit and they may have booked or taken flights to get to the area – if this is the case, consider reimbursing them for their financial outlays due to the cancellation.

While we're on the subject of laying out expectations very clearly, it's also important to discuss with the house-sitter any rules you have in relation to your property. If you live in an eco-house with rain water usage, septic tanks or solar-powered electricity, you should be proud enough to shout about it – make this a feature on your profile so that you attract the right kind of sitter; they will be amazed at what you've created, and will only apply if they can be frugal with your resources, and take care of what they put down the drains. Tell them if you want only eco-friendly toiletries to be used. All of these things are usually fine if you discuss it with the house-sitter in advance but may be a shock if they turn up unprepared.

Similarly, if your property is really off-grid or remote, warn people in advance; lone sitters or first-time sitters may not want to apply due to their own needs or concerns. Likewise, if they need to have a constant or high-speed wi-fi connection to work remotely and you don't inform them that there is no signal or very poor internet at the property, you may cause them loss of earnings through unpaid leave they are forced to take during the house-sit.

If you know that there will be noise from building works whilst you are away, let the house-sitter know about this prior to the agreement of the sit. It doesn't matter whether the works are being done at your house, at a neighbour's house or are big roadworks nearby; honesty is the best policy and the sitter will thank you for it.

My Favourite Housesits So Far

If opportunity doesn't knock, build a door. Milton Berle

We have enjoyed each and every one of our housesits, be they short or long, near to our home town or further afield, city centre or rurally isolated, UK or overseas. But there have been a few that have stuck with me and when I think of my favourites, they quite quickly come to mind.

Castrop-Rauxel, Germany

In a small city in the eastern part of the Ruhr area in Germany there is a house which contains all my favourite things. These things are of course, the sweetest cats known to humankind, named Kali, Bal and Ivan. This housesit is memorable for many other things as well as the gorgeous kitties. Snug, warm and kept cosy with super-efficient underfloor heating combined with other modern German engineering, the house was our haven throughout most of January where it was cold and snowing for our entire stay. We felt really energised during this stay which is a big thing as January is such a down-in-the-dumps month for us usually. The house had a calming effect on us, and we felt almost as if we were spending each day and night at a wellness retreat suited entirely to our needs. This may have been because the cats were very easy to look after, provided much needed cuddles and company and we were able to go on long hikes without any second thoughts (usually we take a dog, or are concerned if we leave a pet at home for too long). We were able to walk each and every day in the beautiful countryside near to the house and felt very connected to the ground upon which we trod; virgin ground for us, but a sacred part of our journey as housesitters. The ground was holding us up; bearing our weight. We were gifted with clear blue skies which combined with the snow and ice to create a magical atmosphere. The cats at this sit were the most chilled out pets we've ever looked after, all of them getting their allotted renowned twenty hour a day snoozes in, and ensuring the aura of the house was one of quiet serenity.

Blockley

Hiding tucked away between Chipping Campden and Moreton-in-Marsh, Blockley is a charming Cotswolds village, boasting two pubs and a fantastic locally run café with a focus on low food miles, inventive chef-like dishes and fantastic flavour; with no pretentiousness. There is a small shop with post office, a village green with children's park, a bowls club and a church built in approximately 1180 and used to film Father Brown. For this housesit we looked after a gorgeous cat; she was cuddly and great company. We were staying centrally in the village and close to all of the aforementioned points of interest. The home was cosy with a wood burner, office space and lovely garden; there were great views from the back of the house. We loved the location of this housesit – visiting nearby Batsford Arboretum, Broadway tower and several country pubs whilst we were here. The best thing about this housesit was the sheer number of nearby walks to discover; with footpaths going all over the village in various directions, we walked for miles with crisp newly fallen autumn leaves underfoot and spotted deer, birds of prey, rabbits and a whole host of British wildlife. I collected leaves, pine cones and pheasant feathers to make crafts and we attended the café daily for a coffee, cake and sometimes lunch. The facilities in the house were fantastic and made our stay here easy and relaxing. Having had our 17-year-old cat put down earlier that year, I really cherished the time spent with the cat here too.

Forest of Dean

In a dip in the landscape within the vast Forest of Dean and straddling the Wye Valley Area of Outstanding Natural Beauty sits Lydbrook. Our home for our first ever housesit and a big deal for us; two lovely people had trusted us with their home and menagerie of pets when we had zero reviews. The cottage was home to four dogs and a cat, it had chickens in the garden along with numerous visits from birds to the several feeders outside. The dogs were wildly different breeds; a Jack Russell-Dachshund cross, a Labrador-Pointer cross, a Chihuahua-Alsatian cross and a Chihuahua-Podenco cross. They were a range of ages and all had very individual personalities. The cottage was a haven to us; it had no TV, limited signal, an open fire and was very cosy for a winter stay. The outside decking had a view of the surrounding valley, the garden and down towards the village at the bottom of the hill. Watching the birds come and visit the feeders on the decking was something I could have done for days on end. Nearby walks in the surrounding area were leafy frosty jaunts in the Forest or along footpaths to warm and welcoming pubs. On one particularly sunny day we walked to the River Wye and then along its banks until we reached Symmonds Yat, stopping for a coffee before completing the loop back through English Bicknor. A great location and fantastic pets.

Little Washbourne

One of England's oldest hamlets, Little Washbourne comprises of a few homes and a tiny but historically important church, first mentioned in text in 1240 (the exact construction date is unknown) and our stay here was a peaceful reprieve from busy life. With fields on most sides of the house, walks took us across villages such as Alderton and Alstone and over hills to

Dumbleton. We cared for two dogs here; a fox red Labrador puppy who was all energy and a 12 year old worldly Beagle, as well as a cat, chickens and four sheep. The house was beautifully decorated with a good mix of stylish and lived in and we felt relaxed and at home during our stay. The garden was well manicured and we loved sitting outside and watching the wildlife; foxes, rabbits and constant birds visiting the feeders. There was one woodpecker in particular who visited twice a day like clockwork. Staying here was nice because we weren't too far from our family and friends in Gloucester and I was still working for the police but the commute wasn't too bad; the home was nestled in countryside but only ten minutes' drive from the M5. Mostly we felt a strong sense of contentment whilst looking after this home and its host of gorgeous pets.

Rural Somerset

This housesit was in a place I'd never heard of before, in the depths of South Somerset in a beautiful rural location. I actually don't think I'd heard of any of the nearby towns or villages either. The closest I'd ever been to this part of the world before would have been the services on the M5 at Bridgwater, and that was a good half an hour away. Hidden away in Somerset's splendid countryside, the village we stayed in has a population of around 150 people. It hosts a church with a very striking tower as well as plenty of good walking trails and footpaths. Here we looked after two delightful cocker spaniels and stayed in the stables adjoining the house which had been converted to homely guest accommodation. Walks were from the garden or from the village and spanned vast surrounding fields and country lanes. There were several good pubs a 5 or 10 minute drive away and we whiled away our weekends by walking to them with our four legged companions to have a few drinks. We fell in love with these dogs and felt as if they had become our family in our short two week stay. Although a new feeling for us having both grown up in a city, the isolation from society was refreshing and much needed for self-development and book writing!

Rural Rutland

We stayed in a lovely home in rural Rutland over the Jubilee Bank Holiday weekend in June 2022. The house we were looking after was on a large farm and we were there to care for a fox-red Labrador puppy and a very self-sufficient cat. We could walk the dog from the front door through several fields for ease but also strayed away from the house to walk around Rutland Water and Stamford. The home we were staying in was large but each room felt cosy and warm which made us feel at home. Having family in Stamford, we met with them for food and dog walks over the weekend which was great fun. The house we were looking after was close to several country estates which we visited including Burghley House and Park. The puppy we were caring for was excitable but well trained, was great at walking on the lead, and already had sound recall when off the lead; this made our stay here much easier as we could relax a bit more. We had great weather while in the area and enjoyed walking the dog in the late evenings when the sun cast its long rays across the farm's fields and the sky was lit up in the kaleidoscopic colours of sunset.

Is Housesitting for Everyone?

Take a look at my flowchart on the next page to see if housesitting is right for you.

Housesitting is a new way to travel, and, if you're ready to do it full-time, a new way of living. Throughout my time spent using housesitting to facilitate my travels I've come to realise that housesitting is not only something that is now accessible to all through the websites and apps that are available, but is a lifestyle movement that everybody can get on board with. There is no specific type of person that housesitting suits best; it isn't a one-size fits all lifestyle and the more you research the concept or talk to those living the housesitting lifestyle you will come to see that regardless of your hobbies, interests, travel tribe, location, personality, likes or dislikes, physical or mental health, age or race, you can make housesitting work for you.

As you can see from the housesitting flowchart at the start of this chapter, all roads lead to the green housesitting lifestyle! And yes, the chart is a bit of fun, but the reality is that housesitting does work well for anyone in any situation. To start off, let's look at who you will be travelling with; will you be solo? Travelling as a couple? With friends? Or as a family with children? You may even have your own pet with you. Housesitting is a viable option for all of these configurations (and any others I've not covered!).

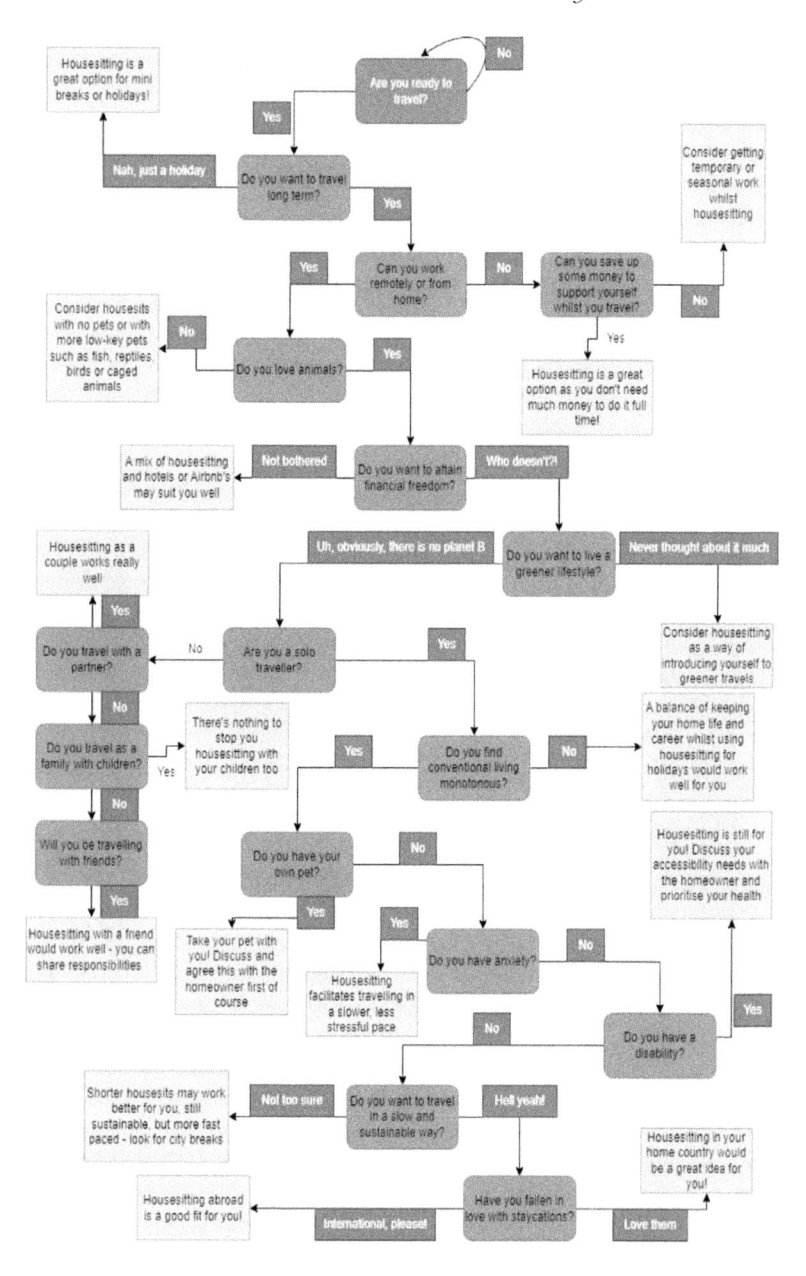

The Housesitter's Guide to the Galaxy

Are you ready to travel?
- No → Housesitting is a great option for mini breaks or holidays!
- Yes → **Do you want to travel long term?**
  - Nah, just a holiday → Housesitting is a great option for mini breaks or holidays!
  - Yes → **Can you work remotely or from home?**
    - No → **Can you save up some money to support yourself whilst you travel?**
      - No → Consider getting temporary or seasonal work whilst housesitting
      - Yes → Housesitting is a great option as you don't need much money to do it full time!
    - Yes → **Do you love animals?**
      - No → Consider housesits with no pets or with more low-key pets such as fish, reptiles, birds or caged animals
      - Yes → **Do you want to attain financial freedom?**
        - Not bothered → A mix of housesitting and hotels or Airbnb's may suit you well
        - Who doesn't?! → **Do you want to live a greener lifestyle?**
          - Uh, obviously, there is no planet B → **Are you a solo traveller?**
            - No → **Do you travel with a partner?**
              - Yes → Housesitting as a couple works really well
              - No → **Do you travel as a family with children?**
                - Yes → There's nothing to stop you housesitting with your children too
                - No → **Will you be travelling with friends?**
                  - Yes → Housesitting with a friend would work well - you can share responsibilities
            - Yes → **Do you find conventional living monotonous?**
              - Yes → **Do you have your own pet?**
                - Yes → Take your pet with you! Discuss and agree this with the homeowner first of course
                - No → **Do you have anxiety?**
                  - Yes → Housesitting facilitates travelling in a slower, less stressful pace
                  - No → **Do you have a disability?**
                    - Yes → Housesitting is still for you! Discuss your accessibility needs with the homeowner and prioritise your health
                    - No → **Do you want to travel in a slow and sustainable way?**
                      - Not too sure → Shorter housesits may work better for you, still sustainable, but more fast paced - look for city breaks
                      - Hell yeah! → **Have you fallen in love with staycations?**
                        - International, please! → Housesitting abroad is a good fit for you!
                        - Love them → Housesitting in your home country would be a great idea for you!
              - No → A balance of keeping your home life and career whilst using housesitting for holidays would work well for you
          - Never thought about it much → Consider housesitting as a way of introducing yourself to greener travels

The Solo Traveller

For a solo traveller, housesitting allows a mode of travel which is perhaps more laid back, secure and slower than traditional backpacking. It also provides you with home comforts which you wouldn't get from a hostel, hotel or Airbnb. Housesitting may appeal to the solo traveller as it immediately connects you with a local person – the homeowner themselves. And if you are planning to go to a new city abroad, the homeowner may be able to give you advice on safety, culture, the local area and of course the best bars and restaurants! For a solo traveller, talking to the homeowner about these things is a great way to ingratiate yourself into the process and form connections – something that can otherwise be a challenge for solo travellers. The biggest hurdle you will probably find as a solo traveller is that housesitting can sometimes be more isolating than staying in a hostel or hotel where there are common areas and the chance to interact with other guests. At a housesit, you will be there alone, unless you have people visit you. If you are an introvert, you may not find that this is too much of an issue for you, but if you are an extrovert or thrive in the company of others, consider how you may combat any loneliness you may feel whilst housesitting. This could be interacting with neighbours, volunteering locally, taking part in activities such as Park Run events or scheduling in a lot of FaceTime calls with family and friends.

Another consideration for solo travellers is whether to avoid housesits where the property is isolated or rural; this will make human interaction even more scarce. Personal safety is also something to think about – is there signal to call for help in an emergency? How far is the nearest neighbour on foot? Do you have access to a vehicle; your own or the homeowners? Ensure you have an exit strategy from the property in case of emergency such as needing to take a pet to the vet, take yourself to hospital or where you would go if there was a break in. Finding out the property's location on "What Three Words" is a good idea if it is very rural.

Group Travel

If you are embarking on a housesitting adventure as a couple, a group of friends, or as a family, you may find that sometimes your opinions differ on where you'd like to go next. Choosing and applying to housesits is something to be done only when you are sure you can commit. Consider the needs of everyone in the group before applying to a housesit; you may like the idea of being on a desert island with a few cats to look after, but if your friend is allergic to cats or your partner needs a good Wi-Fi connection to be able to work remotely, this probably isn't going to be a successful housesit for you. Travelling as a duo or a group always involves slight compromise for all parties; this is something you will need to accept and prioritise if you are to travel harmoniously and ensure you are bringing your best selves to the housesit.

Travelling as a family

Travel as a family is always going to be harder, not just logistically due to requiring more space for all of your tribe, but mentally, physically and emotionally. Children are very resilient and can thrive in the right conditions while living on the road; prioritise their development and ensure that you can home-school them effectively, get access to online lessons if necessary, or have schoolwork sent to them by post. Home-schooling isn't for everyone but a lot more parents recently had the opportunity to master it during the pandemic, so will know whether or not they'd voluntarily commit to more of it!

You may feel that taking children away from interactions with their friends or other children within the family will have a negative impact on them, but if you want to undertake a full-time housesitting lifestyle, you can look for longer sits so that they can settle into areas more fully and make connections with other children. I've seen housesits available for up to five years, so anything is possible if you really want to make it work.

Is Housesitting for Everyone?

People travelling with pets

If you are taking your own pet with you when you go housesitting, discuss this at length with the homeowner beforehand and suggest that your pet meet their pets prior to the start date of the sit, as many times as possible, to get them used to one another. Due to this you may find it easier to look for house-sits not too far from where you are currently based so that interaction beforehand is easier. There are housesitting websites out there which allow you to select a filter if you are bringing a pet with you so you may find specific websites more suitable for you. As already mentioned, there are housesits out there that are "pet-free" meaning you won't have any of the homeowners' pets to look after and so these set-ups could be perfect for you if you have your own pet to consider. There are also several housesits with pets which require less care than dogs or cats, such as fish tanks or ponds, lizards or amphibians in tanks, and birds or rabbits which are predominantly caged. These housesits may work well for you if you are travelling with your own pet. N.B. Don't forget to think about whether your pet would be a little too interested in any of these animals; you don't want any pet injuries or deaths on your hands!

Disability

If you have a disability, physical or mental, housesitting is still a great option for you to travel short or long term. Discuss your accessibility needs with the homeowner before you arrive so that it is clear; communication is fundamental to ensuring you have a comfortable time at the housesit. Don't bend yourself to fit the housesit or the homeowner, make sure you prioritise your health needs and find the best housesit for you. This way, you will be at your best during your stay there. The homeowner is the only one who can realistically provide you with the information you will need to decide if the sit is right for you – such as wheelchair access, downstairs facilities, whether there are loud noises nearby such as building works etc. If you have a condition that means you can only walk short distances, will the pets be ok with short walks? There may be a lot of things to consider when you start housesitting but don't let this put you off or overwhelm you. If you feel that housesitting would unlock doors for you, or provide you with the freedom, adventure, or independence that you crave, then it's time to give it a go.

Housesitting suits all ages

Housesitting is suitable for people of any age, be that young adults who are studying or working remotely, people of any age who are fully qualified and settled in jobs but can work from home, or older adults who are retired or working part time. If you are able to work from anywhere, perhaps with an internet connection being the only requirement, then you will already be aware of the term "digital nomad" and the freedom that this lifestyle grants you. If you are studying through an online university you can often do this from anywhere as long as you have access to your course materials; however, sometimes there are government stipulations that require you to stay in a specific country, so be sure to check this first. If you are retired and living off a pension or savings, you will have a certain freedom to travel unrestricted and you may find that housesitting provides you with a much more comfortable way of travelling – you don't need to lug a backpack, slum it in a hostel dorm room or live without a dishwasher if you don't want to. This can be a much more attractive prospect; adventure and exploration in a home-from-home setting. A lot of people are now looking for new adventures at an older age; we are an ageing population and this means that we are healthier at older ages than we ever have been before. Housesitting could be the adventure you're looking for!

What personality is needed for housesitting?

There is no one personality type that is best suited to housesitting. You may be chatty or quiet, creative or practical, hands on or laid back, outdoorsy or a homebody. It's true that somebody who's a "homebody" might seem like a bad fit for travelling in this way, but I'm advising homebodies to give it a

Is Housesitting for Everyone?

try. While housesitting you can choose to stay indoors as much as you like (provided the pets have been exercised!), you don't have to be out hiking in your spare time, and you can relax at the house if that's more your thing. The point I'm trying to make is that housesitting is what you want it to be – you can offer to do someone's gardening while they're away or harvest crops if you've got experience. You can repair fences or undertake home repairs (with permission of course), or you can simply take care of the pets, keep the home in a clean and tidy condition and spend the rest of the time relaxing ... or reading, or knitting, or chatting to friends. Or maybe you could get started on that book you've always wanted to write.

Common Issues while Housesitting

Every great move forward in your life begins with a leap of faith; a step into the unknown. Brian Tracy

There are always going to be teething issues when you start a new lifestyle, be that getting your packing right, taking a good amount of clothes and toiletries and essentials, or choosing a location which suits you best; rural countryside, beachfront or city. It may be that you have a car with you and when you go overseas you are driving on the other side of the road; something that you will get used to the more you do it. Or you may find that you do a few short housesits and decide that longer housesits would work better; less packing and unpacking. These are minor things when you look at the bigger picture.

Having spent a lot of my life living on the road, and nearly a year spent housesitting almost full-time, I've come across a whole host of new issues that I thought I'd bring to your attention. These are primarily linked to being a resident in one country and travelling through several others with no fixed abode. They are not "new" issues in the travelling world, but they have newly arisen for me and so I thought it may be helpful to other people looking to embark on this journey if I mention them.

Getting post

When we first began housesitting, getting post became a bit of an issue. We were never at one housesit long enough to pay for a redirection service, and although most of our post now went to Tom's parents' house, we weren't really keen for them to open every letter to tell us what was in it. We were also still getting some post to our old address where our tenants now lived which was slipping through the net somehow. We weren't in our home city often enough to pick up post regularly and still find this is a minor issue now. If you have important correspondence arriving via post, consider getting a PO box or regularly returning to a fixed address – perhaps that of a family member or friend – where you can collect it.

Voting

One thing that proved to be a massive issue for us, taking what seemed like an age to sort out, was our right to vote. Due to renting out our house out permanently, we changed our address to Tom's parents' home to ensure that we would receive any post sent to us. We then applied to do postal votes so that we could still vote while we were outside the UK. Voting is very important to me and so I wanted to make sure that I could have my say wherever I was residing. But this simple matter became a big issue for me having recently got married and changing my name. The county council said they couldn't confirm my identity and that I would have to come into the council in person with two types of ID showing both my married name and new address. Suffice to say that wasn't an option – my driving licence had my married name but our old address, my passport had my maiden name on still, and I had no recent bills with the new address on, as we hadn't been paying bills at that address. It was a right pickle to sort out and took nearly 9 months during which I sent off photocopies of all forms of ID, my marriage certificate, wrote endless emails and letters and pleaded with the council. Eventually they decided that they could verify my identity and I am now the proud participant of a postal voting system!

Visas

Before applying for a housesit overseas, you'll need to check whether or not you'll need a visa to enter and stay in that country. This has recently changed for all UK citizens after our withdrawal from the EU; we can now only stay for 90 days in any 180-day period in the EU – which makes things much more complicated. Many countries on different continents also require visas – but they are also usually only required if you intend to stay for longer than a month or three months – so be sure to check the requirements. Homeowners may be able to provide you with an invitation letter to explain why you need a visa for a certain length of time; this will help with your visa application and probably mean it's more likely to be granted.

Passports

Passport validity is another thing you need to check before you travel – a lot of places won't let you enter the country unless you have at least six months left on your passport from the date of arrival. We've also heard of people having issues entering countries when they have no onward travel booked. For example, travelling on a one-way ticket is something that some border security and passport control officials seem to take umbrage to. Be aware of this, and check the government information relating to that country beforehand.

Vaccinations

Another big thing to think about is whether or not you need vaccinations to visit a certain country. For example, for our sit to Kenya we will need to have a Yellow Fever vaccination and certificate to enter the country; this is usually available for around £75 and lasts for your whole lifetime. Do your research on the vaccination requirements before you fully commit to the housesit. Be open with the homeowner; if you need time to check what you need or whether your current vaccination status is enough, tell them!

Car or van insurance

If you're travelling with a vehicle, you'll need to check whether you are covered for overseas travel. Most insurance companies in the UK and Ireland allow for travel on the continent for a period of between 30 and 90 days at no extra cost – although you will need to inform them of your intent to travel. You may be granted cover for longer periods, as long as you can give them a return date, and are travelling for work or family commitments rather than purely for leisure. Of course ideally, as discussed in other sections, you'll be traveling in ways that produce less carbon – or with an electric vehicle. In the latter case, careful planning for charging points will be needed when covering longer distances. If you intend keep your ordinary car with you for longer than 3 months, then you may need to seek out specialist expat insurance companies, or get insurance in the country where you will be staying. If you own a camper van, then it's a little easier; as long as you have a permanent address in the country where you are getting insured. In this case, the insurance package usually covers unlimited travel on the continent as standard.

Self-care and health issues

As a woman, I have suffered with period pain and irregular periods since I was a young teen. Since realising just how nomadic I want to live, and the fact that I don't want children, I have also had to consider contraception methods whilst on the road. I have not reached menopause yet, but it is something I have thought about which must also be a consideration for female travellers. These issues are not very widely or openly discussed in society and although they are becoming more acceptable to talk about, I have never read them being discussed in any travel book or seen it discussed on any travel programme at length.

For women, periods are (usually) a regular occurrence and something that must be considered when travelling. Whether you use pads, tampons, or a menstrual cup, you will need to think about whether replacement supplies will be available in the country you are travelling to. And, if you will be on the road a lot, disposing of pads or tampons in a hygienic and environmentally friendly way can be tricky. A menstrual cup is a good solution if your body can get on board with them as they are reusable and washable. This makes them the most sustainable option and they are the best value for money as you don't need to buy new supplies while on the road. These won't be for everyone though, so think about what works best for your body and how you will continue to ensure you are comfortable during your period.

Contraception can be a nightmare when on the road. If you want to be protected from pregnancy or you are using contraception to control periods, then consider the type of contraception you are on and whether it's a sustainable option for you travelling. If you are on contraception that's working well for reducing painful or heavy periods, it would be my advice to do anything in your power to stay on that type. This is coming from someone who by the age of eighteen had been on three different types of pill, had an implant in their arm (put in, then removed after a year when ineffectual), and then found that the depo injection worked best for me. When I first went travelling long-term I was twenty-one and knew I would be away for a minimum of two years. The doctor's only solution was to take me off the depo injection and fit me with a Mirena Coil which lasts for five years. Although this did work for me, both the implantation, and removal of the device, were extremely difficult and painful and not something I'd like to go through again. This time round, I was firm during my doctor's appointment that I would not be coming off the depo injection and the nurse provided me with a year's worth of the Sayana Press; a device which allows you to inject yourself with your contraception and ingenious for any woman travelling full time.

Doctor appointments are a bitch. Everyone in the UK knows just how hard it is to get an appointment with a GP nowadays;

we're usually advised to "ring on the day in the morning at opening time" which then usually results in a minimum of thirty minutes spent in a queue and ends in a receptionist asking you exactly what the problem is in order to assess whether you pass the invisible test for seeing a doctor that day. This is made one hundred times more difficult if you need to see a doctor when you are away from home – if you are out of the county or worse, out of the country, you will need to research the local procedures for getting an appointment with a healthcare professional. In the UK, you can often join a doctor's surgery on a temporary resident wherever you are housesitting, and once you've done that once you can follow the usual procedure. Abroad however, processes differ vastly. My advice is to do your research on this before committing to a housesit overseas.

Another issue can be dentist appointments. In the UK, the ease of accessing emergency dental care depends on whether you are registered with the NHS, or have a private dental care plan. Dental procedures can vary widely from country to country, so if you have regular issues with your teeth and want to stick with your usual care, perhaps you'll need to schedule your housesits between your regular dental check-ups as well as research the dental care in the countries you'll be travelling through.

Other issues to consider when housesitting overseas

Our first international housesit was in Germany and we absolutely loved it. Escaping our mother country to take our travels further afield has always been a big goal for us, so we were chuffed when we got trusted to go to Germany and look after some gorgeous cats (I still have some unresolved trauma about leaving those fur-babies overseas and not putting them in my backpack!). This housesit went without hitch for us and was one of our favourite ones. It was lovely to be in a small place that wasn't a tourist hub, to be met with kindness from the locals when we tried out conversing in German, and to just be somewhere that felt so different. I couldn't recommend housesitting overseas enough, but longer distances and possible communication barriers mean that there are more things to consider in advance.

It may be more difficult to secure a housesit overseas in the first place. Not only is it probably impossible for you to meet the homeowner before the sit – something that always helped us to secure the sit when we were new to the process – but the logistics are obviously more difficult and therefore the homeowner may be more hesitant to accept you as sitters. Something can always go awry when relying on international transport such as planes, trains, busses, or cars to get to there. As we've all seen over the last few years since the pandemic, airline and public transport has, at times, become a shambles. Cancelled or delayed transportation is frequent and almost guaranteed if you are using a combination of transport types to reach a destination. This issue can make the homeowner nervous, and rightly so – who wants to be a homeowner in Greece relying on someone flying in from America and then perhaps having to get a ferry and bus to reach their property? You see the issue.

The best way we've found to combat this issue is to make sure that we have a window – I call it "no man's land" – prior to the housesit start date. This could be any period of time ranging from a few days to a few weeks. When we apply for a housesit, and have our video call with the homeowner, we always tell them that we are happy to arrive a few days before they depart if they so wish. This usually makes them a lot more relaxed and more likely to select us for an international sit. It also reduces the stress we feel when travelling as we aren't worrying about those delays or cancellations, knowing that time is on our side.

Sometimes the planning and bureaucracy needed to travel overseas might seem overwhelming, but a little foresight and planning go a long way to making for a smoother and more relaxing experience. We've just secured our next housesits for 2023 in Norway, Spain and Kenya – so we must be doing something right!

Housesitting Stories: High Steaks

We were walking at a fairly quick pace; we had two cocker spaniels with us who loved their walks and were energetically dragging Tom and I along as we navigated across a soggy field that was muddy and uneven underfoot after recent rain. These dogs were generally well behaved on the lead but it seemed that this field in particular contained several diverting smells. As we tried valiantly to stay upright with our two bundles of energy pulling us this way and that, we could see the light at the end of the tunnel in the form of a gate out of the mud-pit that we'd been flailing around in for the last twenty minutes. This field contained cattle which was why we'd placed the dogs on leads, but once we could get through the gate and into the next field, we would release them. Tramping through the water which had culminated at the gate (why does a huge puddle always culminate at the gate?) we crossed into the next field. We decided to walk well clear of the gate before letting the dogs off their leads, because next to the gate there was also a small man-made stream-cum-river which was quite fast flowing and temptingly muddy to the dogs whose noses were pointing and sniffing in the direction of the water.

We paused just for a moment at the water's edge to admire the view before I quickly left with the spaniel I was holding to bring him away from the water. As I left Tom there, he was looking into the stream, deep in thought, and as I moved further into the field he followed me saying something that I didn't catch. I looked up to see him turning back to where he'd just been at the edge of the stream. I stopped, noting that he had stopped and was now standing still and again looking down. The spaniels were now both going mad; clearly they could smell something that I couldn't smell, and clearly Tom had seen something that I couldn't see. I went back towards him and finally heard what he was saying.

"Is that a cow?" he queried, turning towards me and pointing into the stream, almost directly down from where we stood. I finally saw what he'd seen.

"That's a calf!" I exclaimed, starting to feel panicked, "it looks like he needs help."

Directly below us in the water was a calf, no more than a few days old. It was standing upright but the water was up to its neck. It was very still, possibly due to shock, fear or the proximity of the dogs. We tried to crouch down and reach towards the calf who was still not moving but clearly breathing and alive, and we realised that neither of us would be able to reach it, let alone pull it up successfully; it was a small calf but still sizeable compared to both of us. Not only that, but we also had the dogs. We'd probably both fall in if we tried to help and we had no idea how deep the water was.

Grabbing the lead that Tom was holding, I took charge of both dogs. "I'll stay here, you go for help back towards the farm house." We'd seen a man in that direction when we had passed about twenty-five minutes earlier. As Tom hotfooted it away from me, I shouted "Don't rush, he seems ok, don't slip and hurt yourself."

About ten minutes later I wished I hadn't added that last sentence. Holding the two spaniels away from the calf – which they had now noticed properly and were keen to get close to –

was proving to be a difficult task and as I peered over the edge at our friend the calf I realised he was now shaking uncontrollably and looking as though he'd taken a turn for the worse. I prayed that Tom would find someone quickly and that we'd be able to get help for the poor calf. I reached for my phone to call him and ask for an update, and then realised that, of course, I'd left it back at the house. I'm terrible with my phone, and never usually take it on walks. I cursed myself and how disconnected from technology I had been lately.

Another ten minutes slipped by and I feared the calf may lose his balance on whatever he was standing on, presumably the banks of the river, as he was shaking so much. He kept making eye contact with me and it was if he was saying "What are you playing at?! You've seen me, please help me.". His dark brown eyes were pleading. I worried that Tom couldn't find anyone at the farm. I worried that time was running out for the calf.

Finally, after what must have been about thirty minutes of standing there and spurring the calf on with positive quotes like some sort of demented cheerleader, I saw Tom running back across the field towards me. I smiled and waved, relief washing over me as he put a thumb up back – I assumed he'd spoken to someone. I told the calf that help was coming.

Just then, behind Tom, a quad bike appeared, with three people on board and a metal cage attached to the back – the cavalry. They quickly overtook Tom (it briefly crossed my mind that they could have given him a lift) and arrived at the gate. I helped them through, keeping the dogs out of the way, and showed them where the calf was. One of the men lay on the river bank and edged closer to the water's edge while another man held his feet making sure he wouldn't fall into the water. The woman got a thick rope from out of the metal cage and gave it to the man nearest the calf. In one swift movement, he looped the rope around the calf's middle, and once it was secured, he leaned down, and him and the other man pulled with all their strength and lifted the calf out of the water.

The calf collapsed onto the bank, unable to stand and looking absolutely exhausted.

"He's been in there at least twenty-four hours by the looks of him." the woman said to the rest of us. The poor calf did look as though he'd been in the wars. He was breathing heavily and still shaking non-stop. He attempted to stand and quickly fell over again. The woman noted down what number the calf had on him and said she'd need to find which female adult cow the calf belonged to.

"You've probably saved it's life" said the older-looking farmer, before asking, "Where are you from?"

I explained that we were housesitting for some local people while they were on holiday. When I described the house, the farmer knew exactly the people I was talking about and the place we were staying.

"You've done a good deed today – we'll bring you round some steaks later in the week." He said, before helping the other man lift the calf into the metal crate and covering him with a blanket. They soon sped off back towards the farm, telling us they'd be taking the calf to their vet and if he survived the day then he'd be fine.

They were gone before we could thank them for their help, or their kind words. And long before I could tell them I didn't eat meat – Tom had already elbowed me in the ribs to stop me spilling that nugget of information, he'd eat them both of course.

Getting Around

It's not the destination, it's the journey. Ralph Waldo Emerson

When you start housesitting, whether you're going to be doing short or long term sits, you are going to need to plan how you are going to get to and from the sit as well as any transport you may need whilst you are there. This can vary a lot if you are doing sits based within your own country versus if you are going abroad to housesit. The further you need to travel to get to a sit, the more complex the travel arrangements usually become, especially if you are trying to be as green as possible.

As we know from a report published by the UK government showing the statistical analysis of greenhouse gas emissions in 2020, when we cut our transport use it can dramatically reduce the amount of emissions. The report shows that during the pandemic, emissions directly related to the transport sector reduced by over twenty percent. This may not actually sound like a big reduction but keep in mind that haulage, agricultural, key-workers and emergency vehicles were still in use, and that some airlines were still flying. We all know that reducing travel is a sure-fire way of cutting down our personal CO_2 emissions.

This section of the book will take you through the different modes of transport available world-wide, along with the environmental positives and negatives for each. Having travelled using all modes of transport from a motorbike in Mongolia to a tuk-tuk in the Philippines I've got to know a few things about the different ways you can get from A to B.

Cars

If you are housesitting and you already own your own car, you may feel that driving there is the most practical option and sometimes it can be. If a housesit is very remote you may find that there is no public transport option to be able to get to the property, and taxis can be expensive.

For the first 6 months of our full-time housesitting journey, Tom and I kept our vehicle as we primarily did housesits within the UK and found that we had a lot of stuff to sort through, having packed our house into the boot of our car. So, we drove to housesits unless they were abroad. When we went abroad we tended to leave our car on the drive of a family member (thanks Uncle S!) and then get trains or busses to London where we'd pick up the Eurostar.

When you are driving, the less stuff you've got in the car the better; lighter loads mean less emissions, as does sticking to a regular speed limit. If you drive an electric or hybrid vehicle you are already steps ahead on the reducing emissions front – just be sure to check that there is somewhere at the house, or nearby, where you can charge the vehicle.

Taxis can be useful if the property is remote and you can only get so far with public transport. They aren't the most environmentally friendly or wallet-friendly option but sometimes you won't have a choice. If you do need to use a taxi, look out for an all-electric fleet or consider using a vehicle-sharing option such as Uber or Lyft where shared rides which pick up multiple people is an option. I was incredibly impressed when I first arrived in Tirana, Albania, and found that around fifty percent of the taxis in the city are electric vehicles. The company is called

Green Taxi and their taxis (perhaps unsurprisingly) are green and white.

Car sharing schemes can be a great solution for you if you are without a vehicle and struggling to get from A to B. BlaBlaCar is an app and website which allows you to search the route you want to travel and find others who are already going to be travelling in that direction with a spare seat. The person driving the car adds their travel plans to the website and can charge however much they deem fit for the ride in their vehicle. A quick search on the website now shows space in a car going from London to Brighton tomorrow and the fee is £10 per passenger – not bad at all.

Busses and coaches

A viable option in almost any country around the world, busses run regularly on most continents unless the road conditions don't allow for it (think Sahara desert). This option is very environmentally friendly and often the cheapest and most scenic way that you can travel to a destination – with the bonus of being able to have a drink or two between busses if you so desire! With more passengers on board per journey, the CO_2 emitted is divided by the number of passengers and becomes a much smaller amount than if each person had driven their own vehicle. Moreover, many coach companies across Europe are changing their fleets to be hybrid or electric vehicles which furthers the environmental advantages.

In Europe, busses and coaches are usually very modern and comfortable with onboard toilets, Wi-Fi and power sockets, as well as cushioned seats that are more comfortable than a lot of car or airline seats. Regardless of these creature comforts, the prices are still reasonable and companies such as Mega Bus, National Express and Flix Bus now dominate most of the major routes throughout Europe making them the obvious travel choice if your housesit involves crossing the continent.

In one corner of Europe however, is a country where a journey by bus is something unlike anything I've experienced anywhere else. Albania has hundreds of bus routes which traverse the mountainous country. Outside the capital city and major hubs, they are usually small, old, run-down looking minibuses. They only depart once full, and so busses often sit for hours before departing. However, passengers aren't expected to wait on board; once you've bought your ticket you can go and wait in the nearest café along with the other passengers and of course the driver, who will all be sipping small coffees and smoking until departure. Once enough passengers have appeared, it's all systems go and the hustle and bustle that then ensues is a sort of pleasurable chaos in which you allow yourself to be dragged along with the group and settle in for the journey (that's sure to be bumpy due to the roads), be amused by the passengers' animated chatter, and have frequent stops due to passengers getting off to buy cigarettes or something for their dinner. Although the busses are usually crowded, they will always stop for extra passengers no matter how full they become. To our amazement, on one such bus trip as we sat there wondering how they'd fit anyone else onto a full minibus, they brought out collapsible stools and placed them in the aisle. A journey unlike any other.

Throughout Asia, sleeper busses are a common phenomenon as the distances travelled are long and the roads make for slow driving. If you are a good sleeper, you will probably enjoy this type of travel; you get a full bed, pillow and blanket for your journey. The beds go all the way through the bus are stacked like bunk beds, usually three high and in three rows in total. On these journeys, there are often stops at meal times with the food included in your fare.

Our favourite thing about travelling by bus is that you get to see a lot of life – you can people watch, you can look at the view out the window, but mostly, you can talk to people on board. We often make friends with drivers and other passengers. Often we think back to funny things we've seen, such as a minibus in the

Philippines where a lady got on board with a chicken in a cage. We couldn't work out if it was a pet or her dinner, the latter probably.

One day when we were travelling across the USA on a budget, we had a long way to travel via MegaBus in a twenty-four-hour period. We had booked back-to-back bus services, and having just arrived in Los Angeles from Las Vegas on one bus we were due to get onto another MegaBus from Los Angeles to San Francisco and we had a couple of hours between the journeys to kill. We went to the bus stop for the second leg of our journey around an hour early; the seats on board are unreserved so if you get in the queue early enough you have the pick of the seats you want – whether this is upstairs at the front (Tom's favourite), or at a table for working on whilst on the go, or near to the toilet, near to a charging point or on the ground floor so you avoid the stairs. When we got to the bus stop, a driver nearby asked us where we were going. When we told him that we were boarding the bus to San Francisco in an hour's time, he said we were the first to arrive and gave us a ticket. He said that this ticket was our "place" in the queue, and we were free to go off and return in an hour and would still be able to board first. We'd never seen this system before, but it's one of the best ones we've come across – rewarding people who arrive first and allowing them to go off and have a meal and a drink at the Denny's opposite, which of course, we did!

With all these positives, what could go wrong?

Systems such as we experienced in Albania, where busses only depart once they are full, exist in many countries outside the timetable-ruled Western world. We found this to be the case in Albania, The Philippines, Vietnam and it is also widespread practice across the continent of Africa. This unreliability can be stress-inducing and it can be difficult if you want to get to a destination at a specific time or have a plane to catch! However, if you are housesitting in a country where you plan to use busses such as these, the homeowner will probably be aware of the procedure and won't ask to you stick to a rigid arrival time. Make sure you start your journey with plenty of time to spare in order to reduce any anxiety about a later-than-expected arrival time.

We once took a sleeper bus in Vietnam which was overnight from Da Nang to Nha Trang, a distance of about 550km. We settled in in bottom bunks opposite each other. It was our first sleeper bus experience and we were quite excited. Everything was going well, we both slept on and off and got off the bus for a food stop about half way there. When we got back on, I struggled to get back to sleep so I put my headphones in and played some music through my phone, which I had in my hand. Sometime after that I must have fallen asleep. I don't know how much time passed until I woke up, but I instantly knew something was wrong. There was no music playing through my headphones. Looking down, the end of the cable didn't lead to my phone, it led to nothing. My phone was gone, disconnected from the headphones and not anywhere in my bed. I realised then that having fallen asleep with my phone on view it had obviously been too tempting for someone on board whom had taken it. I spent hours after that asking people for it, someone on the bus had it and I had another four hours until we got off, I was determined to get it back. At this point, Vietnamese nationals on board said they couldn't speak English and couldn't help. All I wanted was the photos, they could keep the phone. I pleaded and begged to no avail. I never got my phone back, and I never went on a sleeper bus again. Suffice to say, I now keep my phone stashed away when on all forms of public transport.

***

We were once on a ManaBus service on the North Island of New Zealand travelling from Auckland to Tauranga where my Auntie and her husband live. We were going to spend Christmas with them. On this journey, we sat upstairs at the very front of the coach, giving us panoramic views – this is one of our favourite places to sit on a bus and we were pleased we'd secured it. The scenery in New Zealand is famous around the world and we didn't want to miss a single second of it. There were several scheduled stops on the service and the longest one on our route was in Hamilton. As we travelled down the motorway, I briefly thought it was weird that we went past the exit for Hamilton city, but batted away the thought, thinking we must be getting off at a different exit. A second later, we lurched to a halt – on the motorway. The passengers around me all looked slightly worried, and the second that we were stopped felt like an eternity. I turned to Tom, and the couple opposite who we'd made friends with and we all asked each other "What's going on?!". A second later, we began reversing. On The Motorway. You can imagine how worried we all were that we were about to be involved in a major collision. We reversed for a good few minutes, until we reached the exit which the driver had clearly missed, and took it. We all breathed a sigh of relief once we were going in the right direction again. ManaBus was a coachline which provided low fare transport across the country in relative comfort, similar to MegaBus or National Express in the UK. The company has since ceased trading – I've got no idea why …

Travel Stories: Somewhere in the Netherlands, January 2023

It's 8pm, cold and dark. Our passengers were slumbering just a few minutes ago, or quietly chatting amongst themselves. Naively when we pulled into the services, I thought we might be getting petrol. The bus had left Berlin at 9am and we were supposed to be reaching our destination of Brussels in an hours' time. Everyone was groggy and eager to get there. The driver opened the door but didn't get out; and then on they came, two members of border police, there to check our identity documents. Dressed in a uniform of blue shirt and black trousers, sturdy black boots and a black tie, both officers had shoulder epaulets and a silver badge on their breast pocket. They looked quite young (with less than fifty years lived between the two) but their stern expressions and the fact that both of them were bedecked with a belt of terror inducing weapons, handcuffs, a device that looked like a taser, a small electronic machine, a gun, and other difficult-to-identify police-issued items, they managed to create an air of fear as they boarded the bus.

Although I was surprised that they were conducting these checks at the open borders of mainland Europe, I was not concerned; I scrambled around in my bag for my passport and had it ready on the photo page. I'm a bit of a goody two-shoes in that way, always trying to be extra helpful. The border police officials split up, the female officer headed for the back row and the male officer started his checks from the front. We had the fortune of being sat almost smack bang in the middle of the bus which meant that I could easily eavesdrop on conversations between passengers and the border police at both ends of the vehicle.

As soon as the official reached the back of the bus and asked to see either passports or identification cards, I heard a conversation erupt that sounded troubling; the two passengers stated that they didn't need a visa but the official told them that unfortunately they did. They had their passports, and, as I turned in my seat, I heard them say that they were from Ukraine. The official asked them a question which I couldn't make out and they said they didn't have a current home base. The official told them that they needed sponsorship to conduct themselves in this way across the continent.

As this conversation unfolded behind me, in front I could see the other official proceeding slowly towards me. He was thoroughly examining the validity of each piece of identification, using a magnifying glass on one person's passport to check its authenticity, and using a digital device to confirm the credentials were genuine. Here was a man who took his job very seriously; maybe he had just graduated from border police training school or maybe he was just the type of person who enjoyed the feeling of dread that he created by his very presence and the painstaking slowness of the way he checked the documents. He was so slow, in fact, that even a person certain that their document was legitimate and their entrance into the country permitted, would begin to doubt these facts.

After fifteen minutes of his careful checking of the first third of the bus passengers, this official reached a man who was approximately 65 years old. We had boarded the bus together and had exchanged pleasantries, so I felt a little protective of him. The passenger handed over an ancient looking ID document which was the colour of stained tea and folded into three sections, one hanging onto the other by mere threads. The whole thing looked as if the slightest handling would prompt it to disintegrate into dust. The official looked at the document and asked the man for his passport. The man said he'd left his passport at home in Brussels; he'd been to see his daughter in Germany and forgotten it on his outward trip. The border official had the facial expression of one who simply doesn't believe what he is being told, but he continued to carefully inspected the document he'd been given. He asked the man where he was from and the man replied, Morocco, and added that he had been living in Brussels for seventeen years. At this, the border official's voice took on a loud, booming tone, and in a warning voice he asked the man where his Belgian residency card was. The passenger replied in an apologetic and miserable tone that he didn't have a residency card. The official told him that he needed a residency card to have lived in Brussels for so long to which the passenger revealed, in a hushed voice, that he had been waiting for residency for seventeen years. The border official barked out a laugh of disbelief and sneered, "Do you think I'm stupid? You can't have been waiting seventeen years for residency." At this, as if it was the punchline of some long-awaited joke, almost the entire chorus of passengers on the bus began to laugh. My skin crawled with the shock of it; the group I belonged to, the privileged western Europeans laughing at someone who was now considered Other because of their predicament. The passenger who was the butt of the joke pleaded with the official and said that he had an email from immigration which he flourished under the official's nose.

While all this was going on, the female official had told the Ukrainians that she would come back to them at the end and had proceeded to check the rest of the passengers, including our own, before joining her colleague a few rows ahead of us. The female official told the Belgian/Moroccan man with the German daughter that his email contained no information about residency, only that he had a Belgian address and in a matter-of-fact tone asserted that it was not enough evidence to be able to enter the country. The male border official then told him that he would be back to "deal with" him in a moment, and that he should be removing him from the bus due to lack of identification and attempting to enter the country illegally. The two officials then went aside to discuss the fate of the Ukrainian passengers at the back of the bus.

It was around now I noticed that a passenger two rows ahead of me was filming the exchange on his phone. I was wasn't sure whether to be disgusted or impressed; whose side was the camera man on? Did he think the conversation had been unfair for the passenger and want to promote the plight of people less privileged than those of us born in Western Europe, or was he simply willing the border police to remove him and make a scene so that he could share it on social media and get loads of views?

As the two officials made their way to the back of the bus, several passengers were starting to get irked by the long delay. How dare our coach be invaded by border police officials! How dare some passengers not have the correct documents and trigger delays! The driver had opened his hidden snack store and pulled out some biscuits to eat whilst the scene unfolded, for him this must be a quite regular occurrence. And for someone who had been driving all day, it was a good a time as any for a bite to eat. The officials allowed the passengers who had passed the inspection free movement, and several got off to smoke or to stretch their legs.

Getting Around

So invested in the exchanges taking place on board I dare not move a muscle regardless of how my legs twitched in longing for some employment. I had my head turned towards the back of the coach, watching the exchange taking place there with keen interest. The two passengers were young males, probably in their early twenties or so, one had short brown hair and the other's hair was black and more bedraggled. They both appeared rather relaxed considering the circumstances. They repeated their story for the additional border official now present; they were from the Ukraine, they had their passports and they were allowed entry into Europe due to the war happening in their homeland.

Now that the border police were working as a pair, the male official appeared to be the more senior of the two and took charge of the conversation. Perhaps he was the more senior, or perhaps his status as male merely allowed him to assign himself as so. He agreed that they were allowed to seek asylum in Europe and that the countries had set up schemes whereby European nationals could sponsor Ukrainians to enable them to enter and live in Europe. He also agreed that their passports were valid and in order.

He asked them, "Where is it that you are staying in Europe, where you are seeking asylum?" The two lads looked at each other, perhaps a little embarrassed, and the more assertive of the two said "We don't have a permanent address, but we did get sponsorship in 2021 to live in the UK." The officials both looked confused about the situation, with the male official asking the obvious next question, "Then what are you doing on a bus from Germany to Belgium?" The slightly shyer young male answered meekly, "We're travelling around Europe." The officials got it then, as did I, these two bright young things had been piggybacking off the excuse of war and terror in their native land to backpack around Europe. While some may deign this decision unacceptable and morally wrong, I prefer to think of it as ingenious, a stroke of pure impish behaviour and cheek which I have to commend. The male official was now sporting a nondescript expression; perhaps he'd seen other Ukrainians doing this in the last couple of years, who knows. But my attention had now been drawn to the young female official whose expression I couldn't immediately read; I was about to give up when a microcosm of a smile crossed her face. She was impressed by their bravado too.

The officials discussed the situation in quiet tones, asking the young men to show them proof of their sponsorship address from 2021 which they provided with no issues; they were still in contact with the homeowners and using this address for post, correspondence and for registration in hostels across Europe. Aware that the other passengers on board the bus were becoming restless and not wanting to hold us up any longer, they quickly decided the Ukrainians could travel on to Belgium.

Now it was just the Moroccan man whose fate hung in the balance. I'd glanced back towards him while the business with the Ukrainians unfolded, and he was sitting dead still staring straight ahead, the very picture of being on his best behaviour. I took a second to take this man's explanation at face value, as the truth … that he was simply trying to get home. Everyone deserves to get home at the end of the day, don't they? And then I spent some time conversely considering that he was lying; that he was trying to enter the country illegally. In my limited experience of the illegal movement of persons they don't usually do so just for kicks; they may be fleeing war, persecution, ostracization, poverty, hunger. They may be seeking protection, kinship, help, asylum or simply better prospects – be those job, housing or lifestyle. And who are we to laugh in the face of these people? We are all what Tim Marshall coined prisoners of geography and those of us lucky enough to have won the lottery of being born in a European country should be holding out a helping hand to those who need or want it, not creating an undignified and humiliating experience for them.

And as the officials made their decision to let the Ukrainians continue on their journey, I could tell that they were now resigned to making a swift exit (now they had held us up for nearly an hour with their checks and discussions). It was almost as if the fight had gone out of them; just thirty minutes ago they were great white sharks who could smell blood, and now they had suddenly lost their teeth and were harmless. The male official made a show of letting the Moroccan man continue on his journey, but not before warning him in a threatening tone as he departed, "If you come to the Netherlands again without proper documents you'll be coming with us." It sounded quite genuine, and was enough of a caution to inspire concern into the hearts of all of the other passengers on behalf of the man.

Ferries and Ships and Other Water Transport

As ferries and boats can fit high numbers of passengers on board, this is again a more environmentally friendly way of travelling than by vehicle. If the place you're visiting has a river traversing it, there are often several forms of public transport which take you across the water. Several bigger cities are putting efforts in to make their water taxis and ferries fully electric or solar powered, such as Copenhagen's "Harbour Bus" which is a fleet of public transport ferries run on electricity.

If you are going to do a housesit abroad, travelling by ferry is a viable option. In the UK and Europe, ferry companies such as Stena Line or Brittany Ferries run between the UK and the whole of Europe, for example, from Plymouth to France and Spain. You may want to think about emissions and do some research into ferry lines. Most ferry lines still run on fossil fuels and therefore generate quite high emissions, sometimes more so than flights. However, speed is one factor that determines the emissions a ferry emits; the slower it moves, the less fuel it's using and therefore the better it is for the environment. High-speed ferries usually emit more CO_2 than slower options unless of course they are powered by solar or electricity.

If you're travelling further afield, say, across the Atlantic, then you might want to consider travelling on a cargo ship – a choice that will definitely produce less of a carbon footprint than flying.

Although this can be expensive (usually between £2000 and £3000 for a return trip across the Atlantic), it is, by all accounts, an experience in itself. Check out websites such as Cruise People, Cargo Ship Voyages, and Voyages en Cargo.

Cycling

Bikes are a great option for the environmentally conscious who don't mind a bit of leg work and a slower pace of travel. You can now get your hands on bikes which fold down into small packages which are easy to carry, store and take onto trains, busses or planes; a game changer. You can also buy electric bikes that take a lot of the strain and work out of cycling, especially if the terrain is hilly. Obviously if you are a bike fanatic or experienced cyclist, then there are no limits to the distance you can travel, although you will probably have to significantly reduce your luggage! I'm not suggesting you cycle from the UK to Morocco, but you can if you want to. In Europe, the long-distance cycling infrastructure is expanding all the time. For example, check out Euro Velo – the European Cycle Route Network – they have mapped out safe routes for cyclists across the whole of Europe including the UK and Ireland. Initiatives such as this bring a lot of hope for greener ways of getting from A to B in the future. We once met a man on the Nullarbor Plain in South Australia who was cycling from Perth to Sydney, almost 3700 miles, in stiflingly hot weather through arid dessert. Was he insane? Probably. Were we impressed? Definitely! We didn't complain about the lack of air conditioning in our campervan again.

Keep in mind how you will get round a place once you have arrived; it's not just how you get to and from your destination that matters. You can boost your environmental brownie points by exploring a city by bicycle. Electric bikes and e-scooters are now a staple in most European cities. They operate with either specific pick-up and drop-off hubs, or with the more luxury option of simply leaving them on a pavement. You may need to download an app to book and pay for an electric bike or e-scooter, but most are straightforward to use and automatically bill you when you end the journey. This is a great way to explore a city with minimal effort.

Copenhagen is a forerunner in green transport options and is also one of the most cycle-friendly cities we've had the pleasure of visiting. Second only to Amsterdam in their encouragement and prioritisation of those on two wheels, hiring an electric bike in this city was just like (well, exactly like) riding a bike. Den Grønne Sti or "The Green Path" is a 10km cycle route that crosses the city from Valby to Nørrebro and is mostly unobstructed by roads and traffic lights, and takes you pleasantly through parks and residential zones.

Motorbikes / Scooters

An option to get around almost everywhere in the world but king in central and south east Asia, motorbikes and scooters are great fun. They give the freedom to get from A to B quickly whilst providing a feel for the road that other vehicles cannot give you; you feel every bump in the road and there is nothing quite like the sensation of the wind whipping around you. Motorbikes are great for hopping from place to place and you can usually get the best parking spots too; stopping en route at viewpoints and vistas is easily done when your vehicle takes up so little space!

One thing to think about before setting off on your own grand adventure on two wheels is your luggage. Driving motorbikes or riding pillion means that you will need to significantly reduce the amount of bags you take with you. When hiring motorbikes or scooters for adventures abroad, Tom and I often leave our backpacks at a hostel and take one small bag with enough clothes for a few days along with essential toiletries and phone chargers.

Something which first inspired us to try out a trip by motorbike was the television series *Long Way Round* where Ewan McGreggor and Charley Boorman travelled from London to New York, their route taking them … the long way round! Their love for motorbikes and adventure is infectious. We've since watched their more recent series *Long Way Up* where they use ground-breaking technology to ride electric motorbikes from the bottom of South America to Los Angeles.

Electric motorbikes and scooters are being developed and shipped around the globe, making them accessible to all. Although currently more expensive than their petrol and diesel counterparts, they are fun to ride in more ways than one as the carbon impact of the journey is so low. Electric charging points are also increasing at staggering rates, and if you were thinking of going somewhere for an electric motorbike road trip look no further than Scandinavia whose plethora of charging points means that you never need to worry about running out of juice – even in the arctic circle.

When we went to Mongolia, we hired motorbikes along with a friend of ours so that we could ride off into the Steppe and have an adventure. When we arrived to collect the bikes, I was immediately told I couldn't drive my own as I could barely hold up the bike, much to the amusement of Tom, our friend, and the hire company officials. Tom himself had never ridden a motorbike before, but what better way to begin than in the Mongolian wilderness in rainy season?!

If you've never driven a motorbike or scooter before, the concept is fairly easy but having a good centre of gravity helps a lot. Although I have tried several times to drive them, something in my brain cannot figure out the steering motion and use of weight for cornering so I'm usually positioned on the back of a motorbike or scooter that Tom is driving. I'm known for looking quite "cool" on the back of a bike; one memorable trip where Tom was navigating torrential rain and mud-slicked unpaved roads to get to Port Barton – a hidden paradise on Palawan Island in the Philippines – I asked him to pull over so I could cover my nice new trainers with carrier bags.

If you're looking for a motorbike tour in Spain, Portugal, Morocco or Italy, check out IMT bike for upcoming trips.

Cooltra has hubs in many European cities and offers 100% electric scooters for hire by the minute, hour, or day.

Trains

Trains are a fantastic way to travel and one of my favourite ways of getting around. Trains in Europe, and to a certain extent Asia, are fairly well run. Timetables are used for trains in every country and they sometimes even run on time which is an added bonus! My favourite part about train travel is that it is an amalgamation of bus transport and air travel: you get to look out of the window and people watch; you can make friends with other passengers and chat about your journeys; you get to take unlimited luggage (and there are usually luggage racks to store it in); there are toilets, power cables, and sometimes Wi-Fi; and if you're on a really posh train there is sometimes even a bar carriage!

Trains are low in emissions due to the sheer number of passengers they can take on board and the fact that they often travel slowly or use a mixture of different energy sources. So they are a genuinely environmentally-friendly way of getting from one housesit to the next, as well as of traveling around while you are staying in the area.

Although we have frequent delays on trains services in the UK which can be frustrating, Europe as a whole has some of the most comfortable trains in the world. However, the Chinese and Japanese bullet trains may have the edge on this, and trains in the US are not far behind. I once visited the facilities on a Chinese bullet train and found a vase of real flowers had been added as a finishing touch to the bathroom – I nearly collapsed from pure delight.

Many cities throughout the world operate metros, trams and smaller trains, providing low-emission services for getting around the city with ease. These services often operate 24/7 and can be your best bet for traversing a city quickly and efficiently. London and New York are famous for their underground trains, but one of the nicest metros I have been on was in Barcelona which has air-conditioning. While traveling there, my sister and I would often go down and get on a metro just for some relief from the blistering July heat.

Punctuality and comfort can be a bit hit miss at times; you may have a fantastic train service in one country only to find that in the next country it's a shambles, but that's part of the fun really. Tom and I often try to guess in advance how many carriages the train will have, whether it'll come onto the platform from the left or from the right, and whether it'll be crowded or empty. Yes we're a bit sad, but when you travel a lot these conversations pass the time.

Trains in China are on a bit of a sliding scale. Depending on the price you pay and the route you are travelling, you may find yourself going through the wardrobe and entering the magical world of Narnia or you may find yourself in Dante's inferno begging for a quick death. Being budget backpackers at the time, you can guess which type of train we more frequently encountered. Once such journey almost made me swear off trains for life. I can't quite remember where we were going to and from – we traversed such a vast amount of the country in our six weeks there – but we sorely regretted the journey. We paid for the lowest-class seats possible for a 24-hour journey. We realised shortly before departure that there was actually a lower class than seats – standing tickets. The carriage quickly became crowded and people that had paid for standing tickets soon settled down onto the floor until no visible section of floor remained. We set off, our bums numb from the wooden bench we were sitting on. Just when I thought it couldn't get much worse many people on the train started smoking, ash falling over everyone, smoke filling the air and suffocating us. Then came the noodles. People unpacked their food and with chopsticks and mighty mouth suction power they slurped their dinners up. This went on for the entire journey. Twenty-four hours of relentless smoking and slurping. I'd start to get sleepy, my head drooping, then sluuuurrrrppp. The noise of someone slurping on their food always takes me back to that journey. I couldn't eat noodles for about three months afterwards.

Sleeper trains are something which I absolutely love. I've always wanted to go on the Orient Express (not just because of my love of Agatha Christie) or any other sleeper train. The level of comfort that you can potentially travel in is unrivalled (depending on what class cabin you book) and the staff on board sleeper services are almost always helpful and attentive. There is usually a restaurant bar carriage which is where Tom and I spend most of our time, and you can sometimes get off the train for a wander at the longer stops.

In 2016 we boarded the trans-Siberian railway in Moscow, ready to embark on a five-day journey which would take us into the heart of Russia. We'd paid for two bunks in a four-bunk second class cabin known as a "kupe", which we only ended up sharing with one other person; a formidable Russian woman who didn't speak English and seemed to be suffering from some sort of cold. We'd been told in advance to get on the good side of the carriage attendant or "provodnitsa", so we did our best to use "please" and "thank you" whenever we spoke to her – "Pozhaluysta" and "Spasiba" respectively. She probably thought we were a bit annoying – trying to get off at every stop to speak to vendors and walk around stations. But we had such a good time spending most evenings in the bar car, conversing in bad Russian, playing card games and reading. And we drank the train dry, well, almost dry – they ran out of beer, but there was always vodka on hand.

***

We recently had a fantastic experience aboard the Caledonian sleeper train, which runs from London's Euston Station to several Scottish cities such as Edinburgh, Glasgow, Aberdeen and Inverness as well as smaller towns such as Fort William and Aviemore. We booked a private cabin with ensuite and found the beds very comfortable. We were provided with toiletries, eye masks, ear plugs, chocolate and bottled water. Breakfast in the restaurant car was included in the price but we also had dinner and a few drinks there upon departure. Waking up to the incredible scenery of the Cairngorms National Park, after a good night's sleep, cannot be beaten.

Campervans / Motorhomes

A popular and fun way to travel is to invest in a campervan or motorhome, or a vehicle that has been converted into one. They have a relatively high level of emissions because there is usually a limit to the number of passengers they can take on board – often just two or three in the front seats – and the fact that the vehicle is kitted out to become a "home on wheels" means that it is heavier and therefore requires more fuel when on the road.

But these vehicles are great if you want to travel long term and don't want to give up certain comforts such as your own cooking facilities, a bed, a toilet and/or shower, and the freedom of being able to drive wherever you want taking your "home" with you. You also don't need to worry about packing everything into a backpack or suitcase and carrying it around because your vehicle contains everything you need.

If you are using a campervan or motorhome to get to and from housesits, and possibly to fill the gap between any sits for accommodation, make sure you keep your possessions to a minimum to reduce the weight of the vehicle. Once you arrive at your housesit, consider using alternative methods of transport for the duration of your stay e.g. cycling or using public transport.

Tom and I are a big fan of this lifestyle and owned a campervan in Australia for a year, living in it full time. It is a great way to introduce yourself to living "on the road" full time and is great fun. You often meet and make good friends at campervan and caravan sites or at free overnight spots. When our campervan broke down on the way to Uluru, a fellow roadie who was parked nearby in his motorhome, invited us inside his camper for a drink and to get out of the sun. His vehicle was more palatial than our Ford Econovan. The good weather in Australia makes van life easier; living on the road in Europe is that bit harder due to tougher laws on staying overnight, less "free" camping spots, and less facilities. In Australia we constantly used shower and toilet facilities on the beaches, but these types of facilities don't exist in many parts of Europe.

A fantastic app that we happened to discover while living in Australia is called "park4night". With the app you can search for free camping spots, filter your search for specific facilities, and read reviews from other van-lifers. We've used the app in the UK, Europe, and Australasia to find places to park up for free. You can also use the app simply for free parking all over the world. Using park4night we have woken up to panoramic views of national parks, beaches and sea views, quaint villages, and have found wildlife tramping past our vehicle doors; quite an idyllic way to free camp.

We've just booked a campervan for a road trip we are going to take through Norway in a few months' time. When researching our options we came across a company who were in the process of converting a fully electric vehicle – the new VW ID Buzz – into a campervan. We jumped at the chance to be one of the first to hire this revolutionary vehicle and after researching electric charging points throughout the country (which are available almost everywhere including in the arctic circle), we booked it for our trip. I am excited about the opportunities that electric campers will have for road trips in the 21st century; it feels like the start of a much-needed campervan upgrade and innovation that will make the great "road trip" feasible for those looking to travel with lower emissions.

On Foot

The oldest, yet most overlooked, way of moving from place to place is, of course, walking. We are avid fans of walking, hiking, tramping, rambling, whatever you want to call it. We do it as much as we can. We were given legs for a reason! For me, there are few greater feelings in life than successfully traversing a distance on foot, arriving at your destination and sitting down with a drink to soak up the accomplishment. I'm not a great runner, but I could walk from sunrise to sundown without issue. There are more than just personal wins to be had from accomplishing a hike; when you travel on foot under your own steam you are getting from A to B without releasing any emissions. That is why going on foot will always be my preferred option for traversing cities, finding viewpoints, and getting to or from transport hubs.

We didn't get much fun during the pandemic, did we? Well, one day, Tom and I decided to take the current guidelines and warp them into an adventure. In the summer of 2020, when we were allowed to exercise once a day, we did a walk every day from our front door. When hotels and accommodation started reopening their doors, we decided we would keep up the tradition and walk as far as we could "from our front door." So in August, in stifling heat, and with a backpack each, we left our house and walked thirty miles to Lechlade. It was a long day, but we arrived while it was still light and had a lovely meal in a pub on the river. The source of the Thames was nearby, and we decided to follow the Thames path as far as we could and then blag a lift home. We had a week of annual leave. By the end of day six, we'd walked all the way to Marlow in Buckinghamshire, just over 100 miles.

Walking with all your belongings, however, is a different matter. Put a 13kg backpack on my back and I will struggle to walk much more than 5km before needing a good rest. I have a bad back due to a condition called scoliosis and having slipped two discs a couple of years ago. This doesn't stop me from bloody well trying my hardest to walk as far as I can with my backpack, but it does limit the amount I can do. Being sensible when it comes to walking with equipment or possessions is the most important thing; prioritise your physical health and take regular breaks whenever you need to. If your body is telling to you stop, then stop.

In the summer of 2016 at Lake Baikal in Russia, we decided to go for a hike around this beautiful lake – the largest freshwater lake in the world. We set off with all our possessions – one large backpack each with clothing and toiletries, a tent, sleeping bags and pillows, camping stove and gas, food and water. It was absolutely boiling. Sweat was pouring off me from the first step I took and our bags were much too heavy. However, we had no time constraints, no rush to be anywhere. We took the hike as slow as we needed to, stopping each day after walking anything from one, two or ten kilometres to set up camp. We found a mountain lodge to sleep in one night, and swam in and drank from the lake. It was a summer of freedom, a slow way of travelling, and no emissions released. If I could go back to that summer of simple living I would in a heartbeat.

Hitchhiking

This mode of transport is often considered to have zero emissions due to the fact that you're joining a vehicle that is already travelling on that journey. There will only be a minimal increase to the amount of greenhouse gas released on the journey due to the additional weight of you and your luggage.

Hitchhiking varies from country to country; in some places it is illegal, whereas in others it is actively encouraged. Make sure you do research on the country you are traveling in to ensure that you don't get into trouble. For example, hitchhiking is illegal in some states of the US, such as New York and Utah, yet in most other states it is legal. In the UK, it is legal but becomes illegal if you attempt to hitch a ride by standing on a road not designed for pedestrians, such as a motorway. This law was introduced for safety reasons and is often the case in countries throughout Europe.

I love hitching a ride, and not just because of the environmental benefit. Hitching is usually free – the driver of the vehicle doesn't expect payment in exchange for giving you a lift but this is something that you should clarify with them before getting in.

We once hitchhiked in China and there was a slight language barrier but we soon got underway. On arrival at our destination, the driver tried to charge us for the lift. We told him we didn't have any money and he wasn't best pleased!

Another reason I love hitchhiking is the variety of people you meet, and how small the world seems once you start talking to people about your travels. We recently hitched a lift with a family in the Cairngorms for a short distance back to our hostel in Aviemore. It turned out they had lived near to our hometown for most of their lives. The people that accept people hitchhiking are often open minded and interesting people who may have done their own fair share of hitchhiking. They are interesting to talk to and one often enjoys many tales from the driver – if you both speak the same language of course! Once, when we hitchhiked with a couple of men in Russia, it quickly became evident that it would be a silent journey as they couldn't speak a word of English and our Russian only extended to "please", "thank you" and "cheers".

My favourite, and possibly quite egotistic, reason for enjoying hitchhiking, is the sense of accomplishment you get once you're in the vehicle. Sometimes it can be a long process – you may be stood at a service station or in a layby for hours holding your sign up. You may have been standing in the rain or in bitterly cold conditions and have numb fingers. You may have been sweltering under a hot sun with sweat running down your skin. You may have had 100 cars pass you, or none. You may feel stranded in a deserted spot and on the cusp of giving up and paying a large fee for a taxi. And then you see an indicator light and the slowing of a vehicle. Someone has taken a leap of faith and decided to help you out. Once you're in and settled for your journey, you feel immense pride at your success. And of course, you make instant friends with your driver as you feel such gratitude towards them.

Many people I speak to about hitchhiking are unsure of the safety of the process. They may be solo travellers, or simply feel unsure about getting into someone else's vehicle. "But they could take you anywhere," people say to me, "They could be criminals, or dangerous, they might hurt you." My answer to these concerns is the same every time, "We all need to have more faith in other people." In general, people are good: we want to help each other, we want to do good in the world, we want to feel that we have tipped the scales in favour of kindness. We can't know for sure that we'll never have a negative experience, but to date, we've never had a bad experience when hitchhiking.

Travel Stories: A brush with the Law

In 2016 in China, we were hitchhiking from a layby, just before the entrance to a car tunnel, where a bus had dropped us off. We held up our little sign and waited and waited. Eventually, a vehicle – I say vehicle, but it was actually a cross between a golf buggy and a tuk-tuk – came to a halt and two police officers approached us. Oh no, we both thought, should we run? Frozen with indecision we waited until they came over. We showed them our sign and made our intentions clear. They gesticulated at us, at the sign, at our bags, at the tunnel and lastly, at their police buggy. In broken English they informed us that we couldn't hitchhike this side of the tunnel, we needed to go through and wait on the other side. "Ahhhh", we said in unison, as we gathered up our bags, "No problem, officers." As we went to walk through the tunnel (a stupid and dangerous thing to attempt) one of the officers again gestured at the buggy. They were offering us a lift through the tunnel to a safer area. Not ones to argue with officers of the law, on to the buggy we hopped, backpacks stashed between our legs, and through the tunnel we went. We had a great time, taking selfies with the officers and laughing all the way.

I am usually travelling with Tom, and perhaps that makes me feel safer and less vulnerable when hitchhiking. Would I do it alone? I was never sure on the answer to this question until last year when I was travelling through Greece on my own and successfully hitched a lift with a family from Athens. I'd walked twenty miles in 38-degree heat and thought I'd be able to get a taxi back to my accommodation. When it turned out that taxis weren't a regular occurrence on the island, unless you were near an airport, I realised I was going to have to walk the same distance back home. It was getting dark so it was now or never. I stocked up on water and departed on foot. I got about three miles into my journey when I realised it was impossible and decided to try hitchhiking. The third car that passed me stopped. It was a huge relief. The family that picked me up were so genuinely nice that I almost started to cry. They went out of their way to take me to the door of my apartment and we became good friends on the forty-minute drive through the windy mountain roads.

Air Travel

When planning your next trip, the first thing to consider when thinking about your carbon footprint, is whether you can get to your destination without flying. Is the place you're going to accessible by train, bus, ferry, or a combination of the different public transport methods outlined above? It's worth bearing in mind that the average person in the UK has a carbon footprint of approximately 13 tonnes of CO_2 per year (or 21 tonnes in the US), but a single, one-way, long-haul flight from London to Perth (WA, Australia) generates a staggering 3.1 tonnes of CO_2 on its own! When you think about how many flights depart each day it becomes slightly overwhelming.

Sometimes, flying is unavoidable. This may be due to your destination being located across vast oceans or on small islands, or on continents that lack good public transport such as Africa, or simply that you don't have a spare five days to get five busses, two trains and a ferry to arrive on time. Not to worry; you can make your positive impact another way. Consider using airlines who offset their carbon emissions, or use efficient route technology and/or use more sustainable fuel. It is better for the environment to fly economy class as there are more people per plane and therefore the emissions are divided by more people – it's maths, plain and simple.

The global aviation industry has agreed to try to achieve net-zero emissions by 2050. Whether this is something that is achievable or not is under discussion. Air travel is a mode of transport that can't be easily electrified due to the power needed for take-off, for flying and landing, and for the weight of the technology that is needed on board. So for now, the best thing we can do is reduce the amount of flights we take and hope that there is a breakthrough in affordable, alternative fuels for air travel soon.

Some countries are putting their own policies in place when it comes to flying. In 2022, France introduced a ban on short haul flights where a train or bus journey of two and a half hours or less is available. The French government is trying to encourage people to return to rail and bus travel as they have an efficient and widespread public transport system.

Many airlines claim to be forerunners in reducing the amount of emissions their fleets emit, but few have evidenced this in a satisfactory way. American Airlines have pledged to be 100% green by 2050, in line with the global aviation industry, and have listed several ways they intend to make this happen such as: single-engine taxiing; modernising their aircraft; investing in alternative sustainable fuels; and moving to lighter-weight alternatives for amenities such as toilet paper and in-flight guides. In 2017, United Airlines moved to using a lighter paper for the inflight guide and although each guide only became lighter by 1.1 ounce, the change reduced their emissions by 2100 metric tonnes of $CO_{2e.}$

EasyJet are forerunners in the short-haul airline industry and as well as their use of Gold Standard and VCS accredited initiatives to offset all of their flights up until the end of 2022, they were the first airline to support Airbus' ZEROe project to develop zero emission commercial planes. They are also supporting the development of technology which captures carbon dioxide from the atmosphere and stores it underground, effectively trapping and removing carbon

Life on the Road

Home is the here and now. Thich Nhat Hanh

Travel Light

When it comes to living life on the road you could say I'm an expert at how to travel lightly. This has come about after years of traipsing across cities, through tube stations, into restaurants and on busses, with a backpack. I've had a few mishaps such as liquid leaks, losing the rain cover for the backpack, and not doing all the straps up properly and realising too late that a pair of my pants had fallen onto the floor of a diner. The worst thing about being a petite backpacker is that even though I only ever carry a 35-litre backpack, when it's full (which it always is) and on my back with the hip straps in the right position, it's taller than me. This is something I pretty much always forget, especially when I walk under something I wouldn't usually have to duck for; resulting in my backpack hitting it and the force pulling me over backwards, ending up with me on the floor flailing around like a bug on its back.

When I first went backpacking back in 2016, I packed for hot climates and chilling out which meant that all of my clothes were lightweight and I could fit a good number of outfits, underwear, and toiletries into my pack with relative ease. However, we started this full-time housesitting gig in autumn in the UK and we are now careening towards wintertime which meant I had to pack layers – long sleeves, jumpers and coats – which is a struggle in a backpack. This time, I've needed more than flip flops to wear – and walking boots, trainers, knee-high boots, and slippers, have all made the cut.

When housesitting, although you will be spending more time in each place, you will still be living "life on the road", so travelling light is essential if you want to make the process easier for yourself. The less you take with you, the less you have to pack and unpack. In these circumstances, having less is much less stressful and you will feel liberated from the commercialism of owning stuff you don't need. Being frugal with your possessions is not only good for yourself but also good for the environment and the sustainability of your trip.

At first, especially if you're not used to it, you will need to be quite tough with yourself when travelling light. When we were packing up our house, we decided to keep some of our possessions in the attic, but only kept a few boxes; a box of books we loved, a box of wedding photos, a box of travel memories (ticket stubs etc.), a box of certificates/career related things, and a box of summer clothes that we wouldn't need for at least another 8 months. My sister came round to help me with packing up our bedroom and as I was putting more and more of my accessories into the charity shop pile she said she was amazed at how "cut-throat" I was being with our stuff.

I have never been sentimental about belongings such as clothes, shoes, or bags, and have never been a fashionista who needed to spend money on new fashion trends. We can't afford the fashion industry to keep going – financially or environmentally. If my jumper hasn't got a hole in, why would I need a new one? And even if it had, techniques such as *sashiko* – a visible mending technique – can rework clothes to make them look even better than they did originally. I much prefer to mend clothes (and these days there are so many online tutorials on how to mend any item of clothing) before throwing in the towel and replacing them. The fashion industry accounts for approximately 10% of global carbon dioxide emissions due to the staggering amount of energy required to produce (petroleum is used to make plastics and polyester) and transport clothes. If you don't already head straight to charity shops when looking for new clothes, start doing so. Ditching the mainstream high street brands and opting for second hand stuff will help reduce your carbon footprint dramatically.

Another reason you want to travel lightly when you are housesitting is so that you don't have major issues getting to and from the housesits; if you're using public transport you want to make this as easy as possible and not be laden with 5 suitcases. You also never know how much space you are going to be given to unpack at the housesit. You may be given a guest wing with its own walk-in wardrobe for you to hang clothes, but conversely you may be given a cramped guestroom with only a small amount of floor space to unpack as the cupboards and wardrobes are already full of the homeowner's possessions. Packing lightly is critical if you are going to unpack in a small space and be able to find your possessions easily. You don't want the stress not knowing which bag contains the exact top you want to wear; believe me, I've been there and bought the T-shirt (a new one, as I never found the one I was looking for!).

Housesit Gear Essentials

The best way that I've found to combine packing lightly with easy movement from place to place is to invest in a good backpack. They may not be the most fashionable bag, or very pretty, but they're actually very functional for any type of trip and facilitate you in packing well for your housesit. Buying a backpack can be daunting at first; they look quite serious and there are so many types with thousands of functions, sections, and brands to choose from. My backpack which has served me well for the last 6 years is the Lowe Alpine Women's Protrail 35:45 Backpack which has cushioned hip straps, side and front compression straps, mesh fabric to increase air flow on my back, and zips, pockets and easy access to the essentials. This pack currently retails at around £99; not that expensive for a backpack that has lasted almost 7 years, and I haven't yet found a feature on it that I don't like. Lowe Alpine is now owned by Rab and all products are covered by the Rab Promise; if the product fails due to a manufacturing defect during its usable lifetime, the company will repair or replace the item free of charge. Their products are also covered by their Keep Moving guarantee that provides quick local repairs, or if required, a replacement part sent by post or airmail. You can be anywhere in the world when you contact their service centre and they will get the item to you. That's some good reassurance for the off-the-beaten-track traveller.

Some outdoor companies offer used, recycled or repaired products for resale at reduced prices. Patagonia's "Worn Wear" allows you to buy used items which are still in good nick, and if you trade in your old items they will give you credit towards your next purchase. wornwear.patagonia.com

North Face also have a similar project called "North Face Renewed" through which you can send in your used North Face products, and the team at North Face will inspect them, repair, and wash them, and then resell them at a reduced price. www.thenorthfacerenewed.com

Vango have set up a project called "Camping Recycled" whereby tents, backpacks and other used outdoor adventure gear that is still in good condition, is being resold at a much cheaper price. You can grab a bargain and help the environment all in one foul swoop! www.campingrecycled.co.uk

Your day pack is just as important as your backpack when travelling, especially if you are an avid hiker. Not to sound like Goldilocks, but you want something not too big, not too small, not too heavy and not too complicated. The Osprey Hikelite 26 offers you all of the features of a pro hiking pack on a smaller scale and with great additions such as a rainproof cover, mesh back panel, and a scratch-free pocket for sunglasses and electronics. It's perfect for day hikes as well as when used as an extra storage bag when moving between housesits. We usually pack our day packs with a couple of clean outfits and our essentials such as toiletries, books and phone chargers for arrival at a housesit so that we don't have to immediately unpack our backpacks on day one of a new sit. If you don't need as many of the hiking features that a bag such the Osprey pack provides, Wave have just brought out a new rolltop day pack which is made up of approximately 40 recycled plastic bottles; they are Global Recycle Standard verified and also waterproof, stylish and practical. Add some canvas tote bags to your arsenal and you have a great set of bags which are reusable and eco-friendly.

Compression sacks are a must-have if you want to pack your clothes quickly, easily and reduce the amount of space they take up in your bag; they can reduce the space by up to fifty per cent. This means you can take more clothes with you and your more bulky items such as jumpers will be massively reduced in size. When we first started travelling in 2016, compression sacks weren't that easy to find but they were searchable. For example, Go Outdoors stocked them year-round and there were reputable online retailers who sold them too. It now feels as if good compression sacks are nuggets of pure gold. We've ordered several different brands online and they have been of poor quality or far too big, but this year we found them back in Go Outdoors for the first time in years and the brand they were stocking, OEX, is the perfect example of what a good compression sack should be. They come in 3 different sizes – 5l, 10l and 15l and are colour coded. The material is strong and durable, as well as waterproof, and the sacks have good straps.

If you are a keen hiker, looking after dogs, or doing any rural housesit in autumn or winter (or all of these combined) then walking boots are going to be high on your priority list. Make sure that boots are fully waterproof, lightweight and comfortable. My favourites are Lowa Innox Pro GTX Mid Ws that are 100 per cent vegan. Keeping your walking boots in the best condition possible can be hard when you are walking dogs twice a day through puddles and deep mud, but regular care prolongs the life of your boots. Make sure that you wash off the mud regularly and waterproof them when needed; Shoeboy's Eco Waterproof spray contains no propellants, is made from natural organic ingredients, and is sold in a fully recyclable bottle.

Another item that I still consider an essential on any trip is a pac-a-mac; a lightweight raincoat which is waterproof and folds down into a small sack or bag. Great for travel and life on the move, the pack is so small you will barely notice it in your bag. If you get caught in a shower on your hike, you will be kept nice and dry in your mac which is easy to remove from the bag and put on in a hurry. They are usually available from most outdoor retailers for around £20-£40. Make sure that the jacket has waterproofed seals, good zipped pockets, and a hood with a toggle to make it tight to your face.

Female essential travel products aren't that widely discussed or promoted, but they are basic and fundamental items which require consideration and dialogue. As discussed in the chapter "Is housesitting for everyone?", thinking about your period is important when embarking on any long-term stint of travel – especially if it's going to be overseas. Finding replacement supplies can be difficult if you are using pads or tampons, so make sure you pack enough for the trip if you are going to countries where you are unsure of the availability of these items. A menstrual cup is always my recommendation as they are reusable so you don't need to worry about sourcing additional products. It is also the most environmentally-friendly option as you won't need to be disposing of anything on a regular basis.

Having had awful period pain since I was a teenager (with some occasional relief when using contraception methods), I have long known the best pain reliever for me is heat. When at home, I relied on microwavable heat packs, but when I started life on the road I realised these weren't great as not only are they really bloody heavy but not everywhere in the world uses microwaves regularly (my sister will have fainted reading that). My interim solution has been to use the smaller and more travel-friendly hand warmers that heat up on being opened. This is not a great solution as they don't provide the same level of heat or weight that help my cramping stomach to calm. One product I'm considering investing in is the "Myoovi" – a small and discreet device which attaches to your stomach and uses TENS technology to relieve stomach cramps. It is very small, and rechargeable, so would be great for travelling. At a price of around £75, they are worth investing in if you suffer from period pain.

Another must-have while I'm travelling is my razor. There are an increasing amount of companies now, such as Estrid, who make recyclable razors that can last for up to five years or more. Their razors are fully recyclable and made with metal instead of plastic. If you invest in one of these razors, it's worth also investing in a travel case for them to avoid the conditioning strip sticking to other items as well as to avoid cutting yourself when packing and unpacking. Jungle Culture is another company who have created reusable eco-friendly and bamboo razors, as well as travel bags, shaving soap bars and razor blade disposal tins – everything the eco-friendly traveller could want!

Staying Eco-Friendly on the Road

Whether you are travelling to housesit for a weekend or, like us, for more long-term prospects, you will need a toiletries bag that is both functional and environmentally friendly. Koha make understated and sleek toiletry bags using fibres from pineapples. Patagonia make washbags which are Bluesign approved which means they are made from responsible and sustainable textiles, they are perhaps less stylish but more functional than other market options.

Biodegradable bamboo cotton buds and toothbrushes are now being sold in most high street pharmacies and large supermarkets within the UK. Note that many bamboo toothbrushes only come with soft tips, so if you prefer harder bristles, be sure to check. Colgate have also begun selling more environmentally-conscious toothbrushes that are made from 100 per cent recycled materials with plant-based bristles and a medium tip.

If you want an electric toothbrush that is sustainable and environmentally friendly, look no further than Suri. It provides a great clean with 33,000 sonic vibrations per minute while at the same time being made from 100 per cent biodegradable and recyclable materials. This toothbrush is certified carbon neutral and you can post used heads back to the company in the provided compostable package they send you.

There are now also several different brands on the market of reusable cotton pads, perfect for cleansing your face daily and ditching the traditional throwaway type. I use Holland and Barrett thin cotton pads which feel great on the skin, remove makeup, and come with a handy bag that you can put the pads into when you put them in the wash.

Deodorant is another essential, and if you want to be kind to your skin and kind to the environment then Wild is one option. Made from 100 per cent natural ingredients, it uses lovely scents, plastic-free packaging, and has a reusable applicator that you can simply buy refills for. The cases are great for life on the move and are friendly to the planet too.

There are hundreds of soap, shampoo and conditioner bars now available from most major retailers, supermarkets and high street stores. These square-shaped blocks, usually sold in plastic-free packaging, are easier to travel with and hassle-free to pack. Being solid means that there is no need to remove them at airport security and they are much more lightweight than big liquid bottles. Although they may feel a bit retro to use at first, you do get used to them. Other solutions to liquid soaps and shampoos include products such as Lush shower jelly. Do your research and find the stuff that suits you best.

A thermos flask is another valuable item worth packing for your trip; handy for those wintry dog walks or wild swims, it will keep hot drinks hot and cold drinks cold. Reusable coffee cups are also a great investment and can save you money on hot drinks at most coffee shops throughout Europe. Reducing your use of single-use plastics is a great way to reduce your carbon footprint and so a reusable water bottle is another essential. A company called Green Bottle have an extensive range of all three products and focus on creating sustainable robust and eco-friendly versions. They are "plastic positive," meaning that for each bottle sold they remove 25 plastic bottles from the environment.

When moving between housesits you may find you have surplus food and so will obviously be taking the leftovers with you instead of chucking them in the bin, right? Great news. To do this, you will need to invest in some eco-friendly food containers that are lightweight and not cumbersome to carry. We opt for collapsible boxes that when empty can be folded down flat and stored very easily in our bags. Lofory are a company who sell several different types of these containers (as well as a lot of other everyday eco products) most of which are microwave and dishwasher safe. They keep food fresh with a leakproof lid and airtight seal.

Packing hacks

Being a well-travelled gal after nearly 8 years of backpacking, solo trips, holidaying and hiking, means that I've had my fair share of packing disasters, pitfalls and embarrassments. This has turned me into someone "in the know" when it comes to what to do, what not to do, and how to hack your packing so that you can best fit your kit into your bag without damaging it or misplacing anything. A well-packed bag is a key ingredient of any successful trip, and the level of happiness and relief I feel once I've finished packing my bag is a little bit sad; but I'm hoping my general neurosis and possible OCD will help some of you fellow travellers out there get your kit together.

As already mentioned, I consider compression sacks a must-have when travelling with a backpack or trying to reduce the space my clothes are taking up on any trip. If you take anything away from my packing hacks, it should be this; compression sacks are the epitome of all things packing for the seasoned traveller; they are ingenious space-saving miracle workers and let's face it, you'll feel cool in the hostel when your dorm mates say, "What on earth are those and where do I get some." If I hadn't already found a higher power in life I would say that compression sacks are it (you can see the gravity of my love for them)!

A big part of packing efficiently involves thinking about what specifically works best for you. This may mean sorting your clothes into tops, trousers, dresses etc, and packing them in separate compression sacks. Alternatively, you may find it easier to make outfits up and then pack, say, five outfits into one compression sack. I tend to pack by type so I keep my tops and trousers separate. I've found the best way to save space, reduce creases in clothes, and make the most of the compression sacks is to layer a couple of items together, for example by rolling two long-sleeved tops together into a Swiss-roll type shape. You then do this over and over, putting all the Swiss rolls into the compression bag to form a giant Swiss roll type structure. When all of your clothes of that type are in the sack, close it and use the straps on the side to compress it as much as you can – while keeping the straps evenly distributed.

When you are rolling up your clothes into the Swiss rolls, you will notice that the practical clothing you've purchased for your trip will pack down smaller and easier than regular high street clothing. A lightweight recycled microfleece or active-wear merino top is going to want to jump into your backpack in a beautifully small bundle, whereas that thick jumper you brought in M&S will fight against being packed at every opportunity and take up three times the room if you ever do get it into the sack. So investing in proper outdoorsy kit for when you are on the road will make your life a lot easier; it not only ensures that you're properly protected in all your outdoor pursuits but it also helps you to stay lightweight.

Life on the Road

I always keep my underwear and socks separate from my clothes – I hate the idea of not being able to find a spare pair of pants, a bra or socks. Not that I've ever really needed a spare pair that often, aside from the occasional torrential rain downpour which has reduced my socks to puddles. Either way, it's nice to know where your underwear is and for it to be within easy reach whenever you are travelling. In my Lowe Alpine backpack there is a compartment at the very bottom which is separate from the main part of the bag and large enough for my underwear-y things. I don't put them in a compression sack and wouldn't advise it, unless you have a slipper-sock obsession and find they take up all the room in your bag (giving the side-eye to my husband here). Another quite well-known tip is if you do have larger socks, or find you can't pack all your underwear in a smaller place, then you can always put these small items inside your spare pair of shoes; you'll be utilising what would otherwise be an empty space.

On the outside of most backpacks are additional clips, straps, and ties, where you can attach things. For the last six years, I've had a Japanese good luck charm that my mum gave me attached to a clip on my backpack; it's defied all the odds and stayed there permanently no matter how many times I've checked the bag in as hold luggage, or chucked it onto a luggage rack on public transport. I also attach practical things to the outside clips such as caps or sometimes even a pair of trainers (use the laces to attach it and tying vigorous knots). I wouldn't attach large items such as this if checking the bag in as luggage on a plane; they're likely to be lost or ripped off and most airlines wouldn't accept the bag with a pair of trainers flailing around.

As we are currently travelling by car between housesits, we have a specific suitcase that we use for our shoes. This sounds a bit OTT and not very eco-friendly, but hear me out here – travel in the UK or anywhere in winter where it's cold, wet and muddy, requires several more pairs of shoes than a backpacking route around South America. I was actually quite surprised at this when we first started travelling in this way. So this time, bringing five pairs of shoes with me, I knew they wouldn't fit into my backpack which is bursting at the seams from the jumpers and layers that I've had to prioritise. Ergo the shoe suitcase! It's not very big and is quickly filled up with Tom's and my shoes. Here's a list of the shoes that I've brought on this housesitting lifestyle of ours: walking boots (large, clunky, proper ones), running shoes (I have to run to keep myself sane), trainers (normal comfy trainers for traversing cities), knee-high boots (stylish but countryfied; perfect for pubbing), slippers (an absolute essential when I go anywhere, obviously). So there you have it, you can see how critical each of these pairs of shoes is to me, and therefore I will not feel guilty about my sole-suitcase-for-shoes.

When travelling by car, we often use a large bag-for-life for transporting any tins, leftovers, fridge stuff and general food between housesits. This means we don't throw any food away unnecessarily or leave it in the host's fridge as a not-so-nice welcome home present – who would want an open half-used Oatly vegan cream left in their fridge? Especially if they don't know when it was opened; it'll only end up being thrown away so don't think you're doing them a favour!

One travel hack which we were told years ago (or did I see it in the film Wild?) was that once you've read a certain section of a book, you should rip it out and recycle it. Unless it's a book with sections that you may want to refer back to, this method helps to keep your bag light. I've included this tip because I believe it could help some people living on the road or travelling wilderness areas for long periods of time, but for me, it's sacrilege. I tend to read so fast that I simply give books to a hostel or charity shop once finished – so no need for the ripping ceremony.

Top tip: As mentioned above, as a rule I always keep a couple of outfits (including underwear!) out of the compression sacks and in a daypack for our initial arrival at a housesit. This means that you don't need to awkwardly slope off in the first couple of hours to unpack your backpack completely – you've pre-organised your outfits for the next few days. If you are looking after dogs, make sure that you keep out some walking clothes that you don't mind getting grubby, and your walking boots. Often when we arrive at a housesit the owners will want to do a short dog walk with us to make sure we understand the dogs' routines, behaviours and recall. They also do this so they can show us the dogs regular or favourite walks, so keep those walking clothes to hand!

Housesitting Stories: All's Wool that Ends Wool

July 2022, in the UK and the middle of a scorching heatwave. Temperatures were soaring to 40 degrees Celsius in some parts of the country. We were staying at a housesit in rural England, and Tom and I were enjoying an evening drink in the living room with both dogs at our feet enjoying the cool tiled floor. We were looking after the dogs, a cat, several chickens, and four sheep. I was still working full time and commuting into the office while we stayed at the property for two weeks. Tom was by now working fully remotely which had made this housesit possible for us. And, the house was only forty minutes' drive from the headquarters where I was based, making it not too far of a commute (or so I'd thought before driving to and from the office in an old car with no working fans or aircon … let alone having to deal with working in custody where the cell block was reaching temperatures no one wanted to experience, especially when under pressure and interviewing suspects, anyway, I digress). Enjoying our evening drinks in the hot haze of a summer's evening we were reclining and almost horizontal on the sofa when a movement out of the corner of my eye caught my attention and I lazily turn my head towards it.

"Tom…" I said, half asleep, "is that a sheep in the garden?"

All's Wool that ends Wool

His head snapped up as we both realised that yes, all four sheep we were looking after were in the garden and munching on the gladioli. The sheep were supposed to be in their own paddock, a large grassed area that adjoined the garden but was very much separated from it with a wooden fence. There was a metal gate between the two but it was rarely used by us and inaccessible to the public. Without time to query how on earth the sheep had opened the gate, Tom ran outside – to do what, I have no idea. He had no experience herding sheep, and neither did I.

Wearing a skimpy silk pyjama set, I decided I needed to grab a layer before adventuring out to confront the situation. Once my upper half was appropriately covered, I headed outside. The first thing I saw was that Tom was attempting to round the sheep using some very interesting methods.

With a small leafy branch in one hand, he was attempting to entice one sheep away from the planted garden, as if offering them a snack. Waving the leaves energetically and almost in a mystic dance, he got the attention of one sheep, who promptly snatched the branch from him and then turned his attention back to the prized flowers. I doubled over laughing for so long that Tom began to get annoyed with my lack of assistance. Suppressing my laughter and putting on an almost straight face, I told him we needed to work together to round them up. He edged one way and I edged the other in an attempt to trap the sheep close to the gate that led back to their paddock.

This method may have worked, but the problem was that the garden was a large area with several different sections. This meant that even when we got them closer to the gate, one or two of the sheep would spy the trap we were creating and either run directly down the middle through the gap between Tom and I, or just past us to one side. Tom spent about sixty seconds full on chasing one of the sheep which ran circles around him. Finally, we achieved a small victory in getting two of the sheep back into their paddock, which they seemed very miffed about. Then we realised we were fools – we needed the gate open to get the other two back in. As soon as we opened it back up, the sheep we'd managed to return simply strolled back out. They knew they were dealing with two completely inexperienced herders.

We were failing miserably and two sheep soon ended up further away from their paddock than ever before – on the gravelled driveway. I told Tom to go for help, and he walked the five minutes to the neighbouring property and much to our relief, the owner – a retired farmer – came to assist us immediately.

He directed us to open the gate as wide as possible and then we walked in a line of three towards the four sheep, not threatening or panicking, but slowly and steadily, keeping an even pace between us. Within ten minutes of the farmer's arrival, and with minimal fuss or effort, he'd helped us to get all four sheep back into their paddock and the gate closed. The farmer was amazing – so kind to help us and so gifted in herding the flock back into their enclosure. He was a sheep whisperer, a commander of the herd; it was as if he spoke a language that only the sheep could understand. The guy was a legend, he'd pulled a Houdini and helped us out of a tight spot. We still owe him that bottle of wine!

In-between Housesits

Going green doesn't start with doing green acts, it starts with a shift in consciousness. Ian Somerhalder

Paid Accommodation

No matter how hard you try to travel using housesitting fulltime and as your main accommodation, you will find that sometimes you end up with gaps of a few days between your sits where you either can't find a sit to fill the gap or there are sits available but the distances to travel would be highly unethical, unkind to the environment, tiring for you and just a downright hassle to organise. This means, unless you have a camper van or tent for camping, or have family or friends in the area, you may need to stay in a hotel, Airbnb, or guesthouse for a few days.

When this inevitably happens, you may want to consider the green credentials of the place you are booking. Of course, this is not always practical – especially when travelling abroad – but you will likely have a better experience if you do (any hotel who shouts about their green credentials is likely to be a nicer place to stay) and it would be a shame to let all your hard work as a sustainable eco-friendly traveller go to waste (pardon the pun)! Research is your friend here. If you're housesitting in the UK, there are many online articles that provides great lists of hotels and guesthouses that have eco or sustainability credentials. A simple Google search will bring up hundreds of results such as:

www.independent.co.uk/climate-change/sustainable-living/uk-eco-hotels-sustainability-best-b1931885.html

ecobnb.com/blog/2021/11/eco-tourist-hotels-across-uk/

www.sustainability.booking.com/

www.coolplaces.co.uk/places-to-stay/eco-retreats

www.esquire.com/uk/design/a36096853/best-eco-retreats-uk/

hostunusual.com/news/view-all/top-eco-friendly-sustainable-retreats-in-the-uk-and-worldwide/

www.countryandtownhouse.com/travel/best-eco-staycations-uk/

Here are a few questions you could ask yourself when evaluating the sustainability of accommodation: How does the hotel/guesthouse manage their waste? Do they have recycling bins that are accessible for guests? Are the toiletries refillable? Does the hotel use renewable energy? Do they have drinkable tap water rather than encouraging guests to use bottled water? Do they offer buffet meals (very wasteful)? Do the staff get to keep their tips (good!)? Is there a way of saying no to daily room cleaning and laundry services? Are there any incentives to encourage guests to reduce their carbon footprint e.g. a free drink if you recycle your waste?

I have found these ideals hardest to fulfil when travelling outside Europe because many countries in the world are behind when it comes to concepts such as recycling, reducing waste, sustainable produce and eco-friendly travel. However, you needn't give up completely and I've found that there is always a green*er* alternative in every place whether that's in Surrey or Timbuktu.

If you're travelling a lot you may be tired, weary and simply need to rest your head for the night. An Airbnb can be a good shout and it's easier in this situation to chat about sustainable practices with the owner directly. And whether you're staying in a hotel or Airbnb, you can always do your best to recycle your own waste.

Before we travelled to Albania in 2023, I thought I would find my eco-status quite hard to balance with my traveller status. However, when we did two months without a housesit in order to explore the country at length, I found that of all the countries we'd been to, it surprised me the most in regards to being relatively environmentally friendly. The rubbish disposal process was lacking in regards to recycling, but a lot of hotels and restaurants were on board with being greener – from their stocking of local and seasonal food produce to using solar panels for electricity. We saw hundreds of agrotourism restaurants, accommodation and volunteering opportunities – more than I'd seen in any other country, and we dined at these places which were proud of the produce they had grown on site. Every time we got given a coffee, we were given water alongside it, and it was always tap water and not bottled which was great (some say you can't drink the tap water here but we always have done and have been fine – if it's good enough for the locals, it's good enough for us!). I feel satisfied that I have been proven wrong about this country which I had preconceived ideas about in regards to how environmentally friendly it would be and I also feel relieved as my eco-status and traveller status were now conjoined again.

CouchSurfing

Another option for between housesits is CouchSurfing. This website was launched in 2003 and is well known within the nomadic community. Users of this website can host travellers in their homes while travellers get somewhere free to stay. Originally the concept was literally that a traveller would be sleeping on the host's sofa, but nowadays you will often get a spare room. Travellers can join up to see opportunities for free short-term accommodation worldwide and there is the added benefit of connecting with open-minded people who are local and will be able to give you advice on the best places to go and may also show you around if they have time. I joined CouchSurfing back in 2015 prior to travelling the world for an undecided period of time. CouchSurfing had a big draw for me that was more important than free accommodation – it had an "events" forum that allowed travellers to meet up with one another to explore destinations or simply go for a drink while staying in the same area. I attended these events all over the world, from Barcelona to Moscow – meeting people who have become life-long friends. It is a great way to meet people and I highly recommend joining CouchSurfing simply for the events function.

Only once did we use CouchSurfing for accommodation – in Australia in 2017. Tom and I had been doing some farm work to ensure that our working visa would be granted for another year. While up a 6ft ladder picking apples, I had a nasty fall and ended up in hospital which put paid to our career as tractor-driving fruit-picking entrepreneurs. Luckily the hospital fees were covered under a reciprocal scheme between the UK and Australia, but we soon found ourselves living in our campervan with no income while I was on crutches – not the best set up for van life. So we looked on CouchSurfing and found a nearby host. We messaged them and crossed our fingers that they'd be able to put us up for a few weeks until I was literally back on my feet. To our delight they took us in immediately. The couple were lovely and ended up being our surrogate mum and dad for a few weeks – the woman was a local vicar and both of them were clearly advocates of helping others as and when they could. As experiences go, this was a great one and really helped us out in our time of need – so I'd also highly recommend CouchSurfing to anyone who needs short-term, free accommodation.

Volunteering
Another option between housesits is to do a stint of volunteering via organisations such as Wwoof, Workaway, or HelpX. These options are outlined in the next chapter.

Volunteering on the Road

Those who bring sunshine to the lives of others cannot keep it from themselves. J.M. Barrie

Volunteering is something that everyone should consider doing now and again – whether it's in your hometown and a regular thing, or a one-time opportunity to volunteer abroad. Volunteering is about giving your time and assistance either for free, or in exchange for food and/or accommodation. It can be a humbling experience and you will likely gain great personal fulfilment from helping others, learning new skills and meeting new people. You will find that you make lifelong friends and connections with those you are volunteering alongside.

In 2022, I went to Corfu to volunteer at the Corfu Donkey Rescue centre on the island; it was something I'd wanted to do since I was a teenager but had never managed to get around to doing. I also knew that I wanted to go on my own and meet other likeminded people. The volunteering was free to participate in (some projects abroad require a fee), I didn't get paid for my work and had to pay for my own accommodation. The days were long and extremely hot (it was up to 38 degrees Celsius on some days) with lots of physical work involved. Although I was only there for three weeks, I made some great friends and spent my spare time having drinks or meals with fellow volunteers. One of the friends I made there was Bente, a woman who was from the Netherlands. When I did a housesit in northern Germany in 2023 I knew that I wanted to catch up with her again and made the effort to travel a few hours each way to see her. Volunteering can result in you making connections all over the world.

Like housesitting, volunteering has become a common way to travel and learn new skills in recent decades – especially the type in which private hosts who need help with jobs around the house, garden, farm, or creative project pair up with travellers who can provide the help. For travellers, it provides the opportunity to immerse themselves in a specific place, learn new skills and meet people. There are several organisations out there who facilitate this type of cultural exchange; and the standard agreement usually involves the travellers working for 5 hours per day, or 25 hours per week, in exchange for food and accommodation. As with housesitting, clear communication with the host before you travel is crucial in having a positive experience – especially as you will likely be living and working with them for the duration of your stay!

Wwoofing

One of the original hubs for this type of exchange is called World Wide Opportunities on Organic Farms (WWOOF). Travelling and working on farms via this organisation is commonly known as "wwoofing". Founded in 1971, this organisation is legendary for providing anyone interested in organic farming and sustainability practices with the opportunity to work on organic farms all over the world. With hosts in over 200 countries worldwide, there is no end to the opportunities that travellers can avail of. In order to be able to message potential hosts you need to pay for membership on one of the national Wwoofing platforms which usually costs around €25 per year for a single membership, or €40 a year for a joint membership. Note that the organisation is split into different national websites – so this can get expensive if you want to travel between, say, a number of different countries within Europe. This isn't of course a problem if you're dead set on Wwoofing in a particular country, but either way, you'll need to decide which countries you want to travel to in advance in order to keep down costs.

Workaway

Launched in 2002, Workaway is another cultural exchange and volunteering organisation. This platform works in a similar way to wwoofing but is not limited to organic farms and instead provides the opportunity to gain work experience in a wide array of different roles. Membership for a solo traveller costs around €49 per year, and for a couple, €59 per year – not an expensive investment. Moreover, unlike wwoofing, there is just one platform that gives access to opportunities worldwide. There are 170 countries represented on the website in total, with hundreds of thousands of hosts and travellers in the online community. Moreover, there is a feature on this platform that allows you to seek fellow travellers if you want to travel to hosts as a pair. The opportunities for Workawayers are unlimited and could range from looking after children as an au pair, harvesting grapes, teaching others how to speak your language, helping someone build an eco-house, gardening, cooking, farm work or building restoration. These are just a few examples of what you could be doing through Workaway.

When I was travelling through China in 2016, I looked for volunteering opportunities on this website. Through Workaway I was able to find a school that was taking part in a cultural exchange – they were providing food and accommodation in exchange for a few hours each day spent teaching children English. Being fluent in English and needing a place to stay, this was a perfect exchange for me. I agreed to go there for three weeks to help out. On arrival we were shown to our room – a four-bed dorm room with a private bathroom. We shared with one other person throughout our stay and other than a few visiting cockroaches, the accommodation was comfortable. The "work" didn't really feel like work; we simply sat down with the children in small groups and went through English language basics with them. Mainly, we chatted to them and encouraged them to respond in English. The only downside of my experience while at this Workaway was that I came down with a severe case of food poisoning which cut my stay a bit short and meant I had to miss a few lessons. I was glad we had our own bathroom (which was a Western-style toilet, not a squat toilet) as I ended up spending a lot of time in there!

HelpX

HelpX is another cultural exchange platform and was founded slightly earlier than Workaway, in 2001. This website also marries up hosts looking for help and travellers looking for accommodation. The hosts live in a range of environments from farms to hostels and they invite volunteers to help them in exchange for accommodation and food. Like Workaway, this exchange works well for local people who require assistance and for travellers who want to gain practical experience, help others, and/or are travelling on a budget. The cheapest option of all the platforms outlined, HelpX offers their regular membership free of charge. They also offer a premium membership for only €20 for two years.

We had a great experience using HelpX while travelling through Australia in 2017. We had just arrived in the country and had a working visa but were low on money. While we searched for a job we wanted to look for an exchange where we would get free accommodation and get to help someone local. We found someone around 30 minutes outside of Perth in Western Australia who was offering free accommodation in exchange for gardening. It was a fairly large plot of land, around an acre, and it needed a complete clear out of waist high weeds and grass. All gardening equipment was provided (strimmer's, mowers, secateurs etc.) and the invite was to stay for a month and get the work done as and when we could. We jumped at the opportunity and went to stay there immediately. The homeowner understood that we were looking for work and would be out some of the time. He offered us one of his vehicles and insured us on it for our personal use whilst we stayed there. We had a really enjoyable stay there and enjoyed the gardening work; we were greeted each morning by a kangaroo family on the lawn who allowed us to hand feed them. We got the work done efficiently and the homeowner was delighted with the result. And with the help of his vehicle, we got to attend job interviews and got employed fairly quickly. At the end of our months' stay we felt good about a successful HelpX and leaving a homeowner very happy.

Voluntourism

Another type of volunteering, is that which involves volunteering for larger non-profit organisations in developing countries. This type of volunteering has come to be known as "voluntourism" and usually refers to travellers from relatively wealthy countries travelling to impoverished areas in poorer countries. Working to protect exotic wildlife, build homes, build wells, helping communities after natural disasters, or teaching a language, are typical activities of voluntourism. It can be a be a great way of "putting something back" through physical work as well as by sometimes paying a fee to the organisation in order to participate. However, the term has taken on negative connotations in recent decades due to the fact that it can actually be quite harmful to local economies, communities and environments.

For example, an eye-opening 2006 study by UNICEF found that 98% of children living in orphanages in Liberia were not orphans. Instead, children in Liberia are often placed into orphanages by parents who are struggling to feed or educate their children – and when western tourists pay hundreds or thousands of dollars to come and volunteer with the children, then the orphanages become a lucrative business model. Voluntourism in this instance effectively funds and enables orphanages to stay open and incentivises the orphanage to keep hold of the children rather than return them back to their parents. This is not just the case in Liberia, it happens in many low-income countries.

Many organisations offer volunteers the opportunity to build schools, construct homes, dig wells or help with water pumps in poor villages. These are all projects that westerners pay good money to have the experience of helping with which raises money for the organisation and helps to build more schools, wells, etc. This all sounds like a win-win at first, but this type of volunteerism puts local builders and well-diggers out of work. People in these parts of the world have limited opportunities as it is, and westerners paying to volunteer to do these tasks (often poorly and with no experience or training) are effectively depriving local people of educational and work opportunities, and helping to ensure that poverty and exploitation in these countries continues.

If you want to read up more on the complexities of voluntourism, the good the bad and the ugly, I recommend Pippa Biddle's book *Ours to Explore: Privilege, Power and the Paradox of Voluntourism*. It's a fascinating read and covers the origins, intentions and outcomes of this multi-billion-pound industry.

This isn't to say that you can't volunteer for organisations such as this, but be sure to undertake thorough research on the organisations that offer these experiences before you invertedly contribute to a system that is fundamentally flawed.

Eco-Tourism and Eco-Travel

The greatest threat to our planet is the belief that someone else will save it.
Robert Swan

A current buzz word in the travel industry is eco-tourism or eco-travel. The key principles of this travel movement are protecting biodiversity, increasing environmental awareness, and conserving the natural world. The main attractions for eco tourists are heritage sites and areas of natural significance. It may be that you've heard about a specific project such as the rewilding of a farm or forest, the conservation of a marshland, a tree-planting project, or a project to protect a local habit or an endangered species – visiting projects such as this could all be considered eco-tourism. Alternatively, you might want to visit a region or country that has made more widespread advances in sustainable living and this could also be considered eco-tourism.

Eco-tourists might travel to the area out of curiosity, for inspiration, and for educational purposes – perhaps to learn about how to protect the ecology of the area or how to undertake sustainable building or growing practices. Eco-tourism raises awareness of the local environment in multiple ways, and the accommodation and the local travel methods offered to tourists also usually aim to be more environmentally-friendly. Ecotourism provides an incentive for local communities worldwide to invest in protecting biodiversity and sustainable development. In turn, through ecotourism, this can serve to increase employment opportunities and the livelihood of locals – reducing poverty whilst protecting natural and cultural heritage. There is a real push in this type of travel towards enhancing the personal experiences (of both tourists and local people) through interpretation of, awareness of, and gratitude for, the natural world and how we fit into it.

To become an ecotourist is to learn more about the preservation of ecological areas and to understand the importance of your role in the process. It entails travelling to (usually) rural environments, connecting with the natural ecosystem of the place, and learning how to help with conservation and rehabilitation efforts in practical ways. These efforts may be on a small scale and/or with only a small number of fellow tourists permitted in order to protect the location from over-tourism. The funds raised from your visit will go towards the eco-projects or research projects that you are visiting, will help to sustain the low-impact facilities on the site you are staying at, and will help to support local communities. This means that these trips are often more expensive, but not always; it takes a lot of research to find a trip that is 100% ecologically sound but the research is part of the fun!

To travel in this way or even to go on an annual holiday as an ecotourist, creates multiple positive impacts. You will meet likeminded people, and as these trips usually involve smaller groups, you will likely bond with them much more quickly and be more likely to make lifelong friends. Your destination in a beautiful and perhaps remote natural area, allows you to reconnect with the natural world, to disconnect from digital devices (often out of necessity in areas with poor signal and electricity!), and to have a truly stress-relieving experience as a result. For most of us who are quite disconnected from nature due to busy work lives, our health and wellbeing will dramatically improve after spending a chunk of time away from our usual distractions. It's been scientifically proven that feeling as though we are part of nature correlates with a positive mindset, and with increased happiness. It's also been shown to increase our creativity, boost neural pathways for clearer thinking, and improve our immune systems. Another great knock-on effect is that once you become an ecotourist, you inevitably become more eco-aware at home – so there is a positive impact to be made all round.

Having read the above, it's hardly necessary for me to explain to you why you should consider looking into ecotourism – the environmental, societal and personal wins are so vast – so I'll skip straight to the bit where you ask me:

How do I find ecotourist projects?

Costa Rica, Scandinavia, Scotland, Bhutan, Rwanda and New Zealand are all frontrunners in environmentally-friendly travel and I'm sure there are many more. If you want to find specific projects to go and visit, or volunteer with, then the following websites are a great place to start:

Projects Abroad

www.projects-abroad.co.uk/ecotourism-holidays/
This is a great place to start if you're looking for an ecotourism trip. This organisation are accredited partners of WTM Responsible Tourism who bring together travel companies, organisations, and individuals who provide sustainable travel initiatives.

Green Traveller

www.greentraveller.co.uk/
The Green Traveller website is a good base for starting your eco-focused travel search. With tips, guides and route planning for flight-free and eco travel, it's full of great information and will provide tons of inspiration for where to go on your next low-impact holiday. The book *The Green Traveller*, released in 2022, is also a great resource.

Responsible Travel

www.responsibletravel.com/holidays/responsible-tourism/travel-guide/ecotourism

The Responsible Travel website has an ecotourism section specifically for you to read up on ecotourism and how you can contribute to the natural environment and community when you travel.

Trans Caucasian Trail

transcaucasiantrail.org/en/home/

One specific destination that may be of interest if you are looking for a walking trip with an eco-centric focus, is a new trail being developed across the Caucasus mountains. It aims to increase tourism in a mindful way, and to contribute to local economies while protecting nature.

BSpoke Tours

www.bspoketours.com/cycling-holidays/eco-friendly-travel/

Cycling more your thing? Look no further than BSpoke Tours who can create an entire itinerary for you and your mates with emphasis on the environment whilst losing none of the fun. New and interesting cycle routes are listed on their website, along with how you can contact them for more information on your trip planning.

Seat61

www.seat61.com/

If you love train travel and are interested in looking at routes through Europe, the Man in Seat 61 is a great source of knowledge in this area. His website is a masterpiece, containing train times, routes, costs, and even pictures of the carriages. You can use this website to look for trains run by electricity and the best routes to take to reduce emissions. Don't miss it!

Sky Scanner

www.skyscanner.net/environment

If air travel is unavoidable for you, Sky Scanner now shows you which airlines and routes are the greenest. When you search the route you want, say London to Rome, it will come up with a list of different options of times, airports and costs. Looking down the list, you will see a few options that say something like "This flight emits 9% less CO_2." This will be based on aircraft type, capacity, number of stops, and the directness of the route.

Eco Accreditations and Certificates

It's worth looking out for any of these accreditations when booking travel, accommodation, or when you're considering taking part in eco-projects:

Green Tourism

www.green-tourism.com/members/awards

If you are travelling in the UK, the Green Tourist Business scheme allows you to search for businesses, mostly hotels, to check their eco-status. They get accredited with a Green Tourism award which is graded in Gold, Silver and Bronze depending on how "green" they are.

Green Key

www.greenkeyengland.co.uk/

In England, Green Key is an award received by tourist businesses such as campsites, hostels, hotels, restaurants, visitor attractions and conference centres who can prove they adhere to green efforts under several different categories including waste, staff involvement, green areas and environmental management.

Global Sustainable Tourism Council

www.gstcouncil.org/

This council is an organisation who review and regulate green initiatives put in place by several industries; accommodation, tour operators, governments, business and corporate travel and even travellers themselves. Their website contains a minefield of useful information.

The Rainforest Alliance

www.rainforest-alliance.org/business/certification/how-does-the-rainforest-alliance-work-with-nepcon/

Look out for the Rainforest Alliance seal on products that have been produced by companies working to create a world where people and nature thrive in harmony with each other. The alliance works with tourist businesses to educate on standards recognised by the Global Sustainable Tourism Council which they are then audited on. You can check specific hotels and places for the certification here online.

Ecotourism

www.ecotourism.org.au/our-certification-programs/eco-certification

If you're travelling specifically to Australia, you'll want to check out this website. Eco Tourism accredits businesses in natural areas who focus on resource use, are low impact, offer education about local ecosystems, and have operators who contribute to conserving the natural world and help communities.

Trip Advisor

www.tripadvisor.co.uk/GreenLeaders

If you use TripAdvisor to plan your travel, look at hotel reviews or contribute to reviews, you'll be pleased to hear that they have an initiative called Green Leaders. Hotels and B&Bs must apply to achieve the status, given out in Platinum, Gold, Silver and Bronze. The programme was developed in consultation with the United Nations Environment Programme, Carbon Trust, UK Green Building Council and the International Tourism Partnership. Accredited accommodations have a badge on their page: a green leaf.

Some Examples of Eco-tourist Destinations and Projects

If you're looking for unspoiled natural habitats, look no further than Costa Rica, a country described by the UN environmental programme as a "living Eden." More than 98% of its energy is renewable, forests cover 53% of its landmass, and it is home to approximately 17% of the world's species. As well as three separate UNESCO world heritage sites, Costa Rica boasts 27 national parks, 58 refuges for wildlife, 32 protected areas and 19 "forest" or "biological" reserves.

Bhutan is possibly the most sustainable place in the world with a carbon-negative mindset of "less is more." Tourist numbers to Bhutan are capped but tend to be higher spending. In this way, Bhutan has enabled the sustainable growth of its economy while at the same time supporting its conservation efforts in one fell swoop. Other locations such as Canada, New Zealand and Rwanda are also worth a second look for their environmental efforts.

Closer to home, Scotland is another area that has, at this stage, a relatively large number of well-established rewilding initiatives and environmentally sustainable projects. Many Scottish estates invite ecologically-minded visitors to explore acres of forest to observe their abundant flora and fauna. For example, Alladale Wilderness Reserve has planted roughly a million native trees, restored damaged peatland and has saved the genetics of the Scottish wildcat as well as reintroducing the native red squirrel.

European destinations that provide plenty of eco-inspiration, include the Nordic countries of Finland, Denmark, Norway and Sweden. These nations have long been forerunners in implementing sustainable practices such as investing in renewable energy sources and making it common practice to buy food without plastic wrappings. The importance of recycling is taught to children within the curriculum, as is environmental conservation such as learning flora and fauna. Going out into nature is common during school hours in these countries.

If you are looking for housesitting in cities, the European Green Capital awards one European city its title once a year and is a good indicator of a city's green credentials. For example, in 2018 the award went to Nijmegen in the Netherlands, a city bursting with sustainable ideas. This city focuses on promoting residents' wellbeing, actively promotes innovative technologies such as heat-pumps for commercial buildings, ensures that green spaces take primacy in city planning, and helps restaurants to use sympathetically sourced local ingredients. Keeping an eye on the European Green Capital initiative is a great idea; the website tells you previous winning locations and what sustainable concepts they have implemented. Visiting places such as this not only supports their own efforts, but it provides us with inspiration for bringing ideas for sustainable ways of living back to our own cities and towns.

These are just some ideas, but it's well worth looking out for eco-projects wherever you're planning to travel to. While preparing for a recent trip to Copenhagen, I was researching water-based activities and came across an initiative called "Green Kayak." Under this scheme, you hire kayaks for free, and in return are given a bucket to take with you to collect any rubbish you see – ingenious!

It may sound paradoxical, but in some places, although over-tourism has occurred, new eco-tourist initiatives are helping to repair the damage previously caused. For example, my husband loves diving and is aware of the highly rated scuba diving conditions created in the diverse ecosystem of the Red Sea. Divers from all over the world have flocked there to see this, with pre-pandemic visitors reaching around 15 million per year. This caused the death of coral reef and the destruction of marine life from pollution, on a monstrous scale. The Red Sea Project aims to counteract this. It is a sustainable development initiative that aims to turn the area into a luxury travel destination in a bid to protect the marine habitats. And the local tourist organisation Red Sea Diving Safari, organise eco-diving training, use 70% solar energy, and organise sea clean-ups. This method of sustainability will allow the region to focus on higher numbers of giving-back and higher-spending visitors.

How housesitting fits in with eco-tourism

Ecotourism is all about being closer to and working with nature, right? Well what's more closely aligned with that ideal than a concept where you are literally looking after some of the world's flora and fauna in a habitat you've not experienced before? Housesitting brings together the perfect conditions for you to be able to practice ecotourism every day. It allows you to connect with nature by looking after pets, tending gardens, learning about and spotting local wildlife, and perhaps working on community projects to enhance natural habitats or preserve and encourage ecological rewilding and conservation.

Ecotourism and housesitting are a match made in heaven with both concepts promoting the same ideas of environmentally-friendly travel and of immersion in place. Previous searches on Trusted Housesitters have revealed several off-grid homes that generate their own renewable energy, focus on reducing their impact, and grow all their own food. By staying in their home, you will be living in this way, learning about sustainable practices, and having far less impact on the environment than if you were staying in a hotel.

Looking for eco-tourist projects prior to housesits is a great way to start on your ecotourism journey, and once you've found a project that looks interesting, you could look for housesits close by so that you can do both at the same time. Just be sure not to over commit to projects that will require a lot of hours if it will be of detriment to any pets you are looking after. If doing both at the same time doesn't look as though it will work, you can always do a month on a project, then a month on a housesit to balance out the finances.

Slow and Sustainable Travel

In an age of speed, I began to think, nothing could be more invigorating than going slow. Pico Iyer

Slow travel is an idea that has gathered momentum and popularity over the last decade. It is a change in the way we think about travel – away from the tourist mindset of rushing to a destination in the quickest way possible and rushing around the sites, or soaking in the sun while taking no interest in the local culture, language or traditions. Being shut inside our homes during the pandemic, and restricted from travelling anywhere apart from the local shop, allowed people the time to return to daydreaming about where they would visit when the restrictions were relaxed. Many still wanted that typical sunshine beach holiday, but for others, the restrictions brought a new appreciation of the right to geographical and financial freedom that they had previously taken for granted, and had them yearning for more adventurous journeys.

Yet, the drastic reduction in travel did have a positive aspect; the restorative impact on ecosystems around the world were astounding. Wildlife reclaimed previously tourist-heavy areas, forests began to rewild themselves, and pollution caused by air, road and rail transport was reduced on a huge scale. You may remember those stories during lockdown like the goats coming

Slow and Sustainable Travel

down from the mountains and strutting their stuff in the residential streets of Llandudno. Newsworthy stuff that.

After watching this reclamation of the modern world by native flora and fauna, I was tormented by an internal moral conflict. I'd always been obsessed with travel, it was without a doubt the very reason for my being; I had always felt I would be travelling the world in one form or another, living a nomadic life in harmony with the environment around me. But now I was faced with this dilemma; can travel ever be good for the environment? I spent many long locked-down months researching the environmental impact of planes, trains, cars, anything that gets you from A to B. The results weren't pretty and I knew I needed to find a solution to travelling long term that would be less harmful to the environment – otherwise my life plan of travelling the world was up in smoke (pardon the pun). I just knew I wouldn't be able to live with the guilt of knowing how much damage I'd be doing if I continued travelling the way I had before. I was determined to change the way I travelled.

Reading up on the idea of "slow travel" during this identity crisis allowed me to breathe a little sigh of relief; here was a concept that might allow me to tread the fine line between continuing to experience the enjoyment of travel while also leaving little or no damage in my wake. Slow travel could also be called "conscious" travel – it's a way of travelling that prioritizes connection rather than exploitation. It prioritizes connection to the local place – to its people and its culture – and emphasizes ways of travel that are more sustainable and ecologically sound. With slow travel, the journey is part of the adventure rather being merely something to be rushed so that you can get to your destination.

Reducing air travel is the best way to start making a difference. Yes, you may be able to fly to Spain in a couple of hours for £150 return instead of travelling by train that costs double and takes 13 hours with 2 changes. Yes, travelling in this way is more tiring. But choosing the latter provides more than just the satisfaction of doing something amazing for the environment and reinventing you as a considerate, humane and responsible traveller.

Trains and busses are also a more romantic, scenic, and interesting way to travel than by air, and definitely more relaxing. There are no check-ins for luggage, no endless queues through airport security, and no horrendous parking fees. You can just hop on, sit down, and go. You can travel at your own pace, often on flexible tickets, instead of being restricted by plane times and having to speed back to airports. And needless to say, for those of us who are anxious flyers (yes, me), not having to put yourself through all the faff of flying unless absolutely necessary, is a huge bonus.

Seeing more along the way – both by travelling more slowly and by spending longer in each destination – means that slow travel is undeniably a more fulfilling and enriching experience. As you trundle by train through the Swiss Alps or the Scottish Highlands, the travel to your destination becomes a memorable part of the trip. You'll see landscapes you've never seen before, people going about their daily life, and small tucked-away places where you can alight, should you so choose. Travelling through the lands that separate your home and your destination brings an appreciation of your destination that you wouldn't otherwise have had. It gives you a deeper sense of connection to the world in general, and allows for the more meaningful memories that immersion in the local culture provides.

Many of us are bound by annual leave restrictions – by not having enough of it, and by having to take it within a specific timeframe each year. This can be a difficult barrier to overcome, and if you feel that it constricts your newfound conscious travel lifestyle, you could speak to your company about how they can be more aware of the potentially environmentally damaging decisions they are forcing their employees to make.

You could also consider whether your work is something you could do from home, and if so, put in an alternative working location request. Many of us were forced to work from home throughout the pandemic and found that we were actually a lot more productive while at the same being less stressed and more relaxed. The pandemic also proved that most jobs can be done from home, unless you work for the emergency services or a job where being face-to-face is necessary. If your job is doable remotely but you work for a company who don't have a work-from-home policy, consider bringing it up with them or looking for a company who have this in place.

The cost of travelling slower is undoubtedly a big drawback for many people, but travelling less often and going for longer periods of time can be one way of combatting this. By going on fewer city breaks (although there are some great city-to-city coach and train deals to be had out there!), you will be doing yourself and the world a favour. Spending longer in a place, with more time to settle into its culture, provides a more fulfilling experience and helps save our planet.

Sustainable Travel

Slow travel is inherently more sustainable. Sustainability means living our lives in a way that can be sustainable for years to come without causing any damage to the planet for future generations; it requires making decisions around the way we run all aspects of our lives from our economies, to our societies and cultures. To travel sustainably is to fully consider climate change, environmental pollution, and community wellbeing in each destination, and to assess whether the overall impact of our travel to that place will be positive or negative. It means being thoughtful about the location, transport methods, types of accommodation, the places we eat, and the transport methods we employ throughout our stay.

I recently went to a talk where Chris Haslam, Chief travel writer at the Sunday Times said something poignant: "If you believe you can visit somewhere, and leave it even fractionally better than when you arrived, then you should go." His top tips to sustainability in the tourist industry were to "Fly less, stay longer, and leave it better than when you arrived." Everyone can make a positive impact on a place whether that simply means supporting local food producers and restaurants, or spending a day or two volunteering in the community, or doing a few hours of litter picking with your family. At the very least, travelling in a sustainable way means leaving "no trace" (whether that be camping or walking through cities), never flying somewhere that can be accessed easily by overland travel, and never visiting places that have been listed as vulnerable or protected ecosystems.

Where to go (and where to avoid) as a sustainable traveller

Staycation

The trend of the "staycation" – of going on holiday within your own country – was effectively enforced by the pandemic. Travelling a shorter distance to your destination means less pollution, a lower carbon footprint, and it's a lot easier to avoid flying – so that already makes it more sustainable. Not only are we supporting our own national economies when we travel in this way, but we have less of the "getting there" travel stress that can be induced by overseas travel. Moreover, we get to explore the nooks and crannies of our own countries that we never knew existed.

Over tourism – places to avoid

Us western tourists have a bit of a reputation for discovering sun-drenched unspoilt destinations and commandeering them to become a hub for western holidaymakers. The influx of people to these destinations increases the amount of flights there which in turn makes airfares cheaper, and so we book to go there more frequently. Increased competition often also means that food and drink becomes cheaper– and if there's anything us Brits love, it's cheap booze. This cycle of over tourism can be the systematic ruining of a place – as seen in places such as Benidorm in Spain, Bali in Indonesia, Maya Beach in Thailand, and Santorini in Greece. In all of these places, it is easier to meet another tourist rather than a local.

The increase in traffic, air travel, or cruise ships, causes air pollution, landfill sites struggle, and factors such as increased sewage waste, suncream leaching, water sports, and boat anchors, cause water pollution and damage to coral reefs. A lot of these places lose their charm as a result. So whether you are staycationing or travelling abroad, consider seeking housesits in less touristic places. For example, instead of visiting Cornwall that tends to be busy all year round, consider the Northumberland coast – all the bang, without the buck, and without the people too!

Places that have had their ecosystems badly damaged due to global warming or over-tourism should be left alone so that they can recover; for example, the Great Barrier Reef (GBR) in Australia whose coral bleaching is a direct result of the rise in sea water temperatures. A distressing report conducted this year stated that 91% of the reefs on the GBR have been affected by a mass event of coral bleaching this year.

Another example of the damaging impact of over-tourism is Maya Bay beach in Thailand, famous for being "The Beach" from the film of the same name starring Leonardo Di Caprio. Due to extreme rubbish building up, coral reef decaying, and native wildlife retreating from the area, the Thai authorities decided to close the beach entirely in 2018. The beach was initially supposed to be closed for four months only, but due to the lockdowns it was actually closed for four years. Native wildlife returned in abundance, and now the coral reef is blooming and rare wildlife species have re-appeared. This beach has now reopened to tourists, and hopefully tourist visits will now be arranged in a more controlled and sustainable way that respects the fragile environment there. But ideally, don't visit at all unless you have specific reason to.

Even Mount Everest has been affected by over-tourism. This has led to overcrowding, safety issues, and a rubbish problem close to the summit – as the famous 2019 photo showed.

When to travel

Considering when to travel to a destination can make a difference to the impact your visit will have on a place, as well as your experience of it. The most sensible way to think about this question is to think of another; when can you give back the most to a community living in a certain place? One answer is to avoid travelling at times when the place will be at its busiest. For example, if you see a housesit near Hyde Park when Winter Wonderland is on, you can be sure there will be crowds and chaos; this may be something you want to do, or something you'd rather avoid. If you feel that other areas of the UK may benefit from tourism at that particular time of the year instead, then look for housesits there. A great feature of most housesitting sites is that you can search for housesits in specific places, there is a map view so you can see what housesits are out there.

In the case of certain destinations that are overrun with tourists at certain times of the year such as Rome in August, New York at Christmas, the French Alps in February, and the Lake District on Easter weekend (you get the idea) – try looking for housesits off-season, or looking for more unknown places. Busy doesn't always mean a thriving economy for the locals; it can actually cripple their way of living as they have to rely on the tourist income earned in just a few short weeks or months of the year. It also means that locals are pushed out of their own neighbourhoods as tourism increases the price of properties, and hotels are built instead of residential housing. Crowded places full of tourists don't create the most relaxing holidays and tend to give inauthentic impressions of a place; instead of seeing places thriving in sustainable ways you're seeing them overrun by the tourism industry – tour guides touting for business and staff in the service industry run off their feet in unsustainable seasonal work.

Some of us may be bound by school terms or annual leave periods throughout the year, which inevitably makes travelling "off-season" quite difficult (warning - be aware of fees that schools are now implementing if you take your child out of school outside of the set holiday periods). The main things that we want when we go on holiday is hot weather and relaxation, and the weather also tends to be the best throughout the typical summer months of July and August. Shoulder seasons can be a winning solution here, when weather is still warm, crowds are lessened and prices to travel and stay are lower. In Europe, this tends to mean booking holidays between early April-early June and early September-late October. Destinations that are notoriously busy in summer months tend to struggle throughout winters and shoulder-season periods; they make all their money in a couple of months and have to survive the rest of the year on it. Travelling outside the normal tourist season means you can improve their livelihood and enable them to be more stable year-round. You will also have a fuller understanding of the place you visit as you will see it outside of the tourist season.

You will undoubtedly face some differences in your holidays due to this change; the weather may be less predictable and you may find certain bars or restaurants are closed. However, the best holidays are ones where you take an unexpected route or do something different to what you'd normally do. A trip to Snowdonia in early spring may not be something you'd normally book in an instant, but it could be the perfect conditions to try out wild swimming. Visiting a ski resort in the middle of summer might sound like madness, but there will be fantastic hiking, mountain biking and paragliding. And how about a beach holiday in winter; try cooking classes, star gazing and spa days to warm you up! All it takes is a little creative thinking outside of the usual summer-holiday box.

Under-tourism

You may have recently heard that an area is struggling due to under-tourism, and this may be a good reason to go. Sri Lanka is one such country that has found it difficult to bounce back from the knock-on effects not only of the pandemic but also the political tensions within the country which has meant that many countries' foreign offices have advised their citizens not to travel there in recent years. However, this advice has now lifted and the country is now considered a safe destination; you will likely find that long-abandoned local tour guides, restaurant owners, and hotel staff eagerly await your return to the island nation.

Disaster tourism

This term has negative connotations with critics using it to apply to tourists who have a voyeuristic fascination with other people's misfortune. However, consider the impact on local economies of the slump in tourism during these times. Regions hit by phenomena such as cyclones, typhoons, earthquakes, tsunamis, wildfires, landslides and avalanches often find that they are doubly punished; firstly by the disaster itself, and secondly by the immediate cessation of tourists. If they rely on the latter, they often struggle for years after the disaster zone has been restored. For example, it was estimated that the recent wildfires in Australia cost the tourism industry in that country something in the region of 4.5 billion dollars.

So once an area is considered safe by the foreign office, you could consider a trip there. You will find that during these times, prices of both travel and accommodation are cheaper and the locals are more grateful for your visit. Not only that, but you will also be making a direct impact on the economic growth and regeneration of the place. You could also combine your trip with some volunteering in these areas, such as rebuilding homes or clearing debris.

In the case of man-made disasters such as biological or chemical threats, terrorist attacks or other civil unrest it may of course take some time before a place is safe to visit. In the case of Chernobyl, for example, it is permitted to visit the area but, due to the ongoing radiation emitted, may not be safe for those already suffering from certain health issues.

Of course these decisions are always a personal choice and need to be carefully made according to your personal circumstances. A personal experience of this for me was in the summer 2015 when we had a holiday booked to Tunisia. Just before our trip there were two incidents quite close together of mass shootings; one in Tunis and one on the beach near to Sousse. Our holiday was booked one hour north of the beach where the shootings took place. Did this worry us? A little. Did we go? Yes. We knew that two attacks so close together indicated growing political tension in the country. However, we also knew that cancelling the trip would be what most people would do, and that the impact of this on the local communities that relied on tourists would be devastating. There is no heroism in making the decision to go, just as there is no weakness in changing your travel destination. You need to make sure that the decisions you make are the right ones for you and your loved ones. We had a lovely time by the way!

How housesitting fits in with slow and sustainable travel

Housesitting inherently fits into the slow and sustainable remit. Staying for extended periods of time in a person's home, means a lower carbon footprint from travel – and if you can get there by train or ferry, or car-share, then all the better. Staying longer will also offset slightly the need to drive if it's a rural location or if you have luggage. And the fact that housesitting essentially provides you with free accommodation, means that you can spend some of the money that you have saved on accommodation on slower means of getting there! By searching for available housesits in the map view on your app, you can plan to move just small distances between sits – which means you'll get to know the area even better, and makes the journeys that much easier to keep. We started housesitting in the North Cotswolds, and we are from Gloucester originally, so we began our journey only an hour from our home. From there, we moved around the UK, usually only travelling for an hour or two between sits. We plan to move into Europe in the next six months and will continue to travel in this way, strategically planning our movement to places that may or may not already be on our list of places to see (which is pretty much everywhere in the world).

Slow travel means more interaction with local communities, and housesitting means that you will naturally interact far more with the local community than you would have done had you stayed in a hotel. When you housesit, you are engaging with the local community from the instant you reach out to someone who needs their home and pets looked after. Use this person as a valuable resource; they can introduce you to the neighbours, and they can tell you about that tucked-away gem of a restaurant, or the local farmer/grower who sells their fresh veg on-site on Saturday mornings. They can also let you know about local volunteering projects that they are involved in, and/or that you could get involved with during your stay. Although the idea of getting involved in community projects, where you don't know these people from Adam, may seem daunting, don't be shy! The people running these types of projects are always up for a conversation; be upfront and tell them how long you will be there, be keen and enthusiastic about the cause and there is usually a quickfire way to get involved even if your time is limited.

Other options that might provide you with valuable cultural exchange include joining in with local exercise classes and speaking to other attendees, or going to church services (even if you aren't of that religion) and speaking to wardens about work you could help with. Chat with the locals to find out more about what's going on in the area, and, if abroad, practice your language skills!

Slow and Sustainable Travel

The hosts may themselves be personally doing things to combat their own impact on the local area and environment. For example, we looked after a home for people who had made use of a well – a natural water source that was underneath the house – which supplied all their water needs including drinking water, water for toilet flushes, and showers. Staying somewhere like this means that your stay will have less impact on the local environment, and you may learn more about sustainable ways of living and can later help to spread the word! There are people out there who care as much as you do about renewables and sustainability; you just need to ask the right questions. Talk, talk and talk some more.

The longer you stay, the more you will feel the benefit of being more integrated in the community and of seeing the area through the eyes of a resident rather than a tourist. The process of unpacking and packing back up can be stressful and a longer stay minimises the time spent doing that. We are currently aiming to conduct housesits of around one month in length minimum – we feel this is a good amount of time to actively participate within the community and explore the surrounding walks on offer.

One argument against housesitting being sustainable is that you are not paying for your accommodation, so hotels, B&B's and campsites in the area will not be benefiting from your custom. Yet, it's also possible that you wouldn't have visited that area at all if it wasn't for housesitting, and you will still be putting money back into the area by buying at local shops and eating at local restaurants. Although money might not be being put into accommodation by your visit, you are still spending money within the area. Supporting local businesses such as locally-run independent restaurants, farm shops, cafés and gift shops, is a great way to do this. The money you have saved on accommodation can not only by invested in slower ways of travel, but can also be invested in the often pricier, but more sustainable, local food options. When you are eating or buying food, speak to the staff about the items, whether the ingredients are fresh and local, and if so, where exactly they are from. Take an interest in food miles and zero waste policies that businesses may have. If they are doing it, they will be keen to talk to you about it and will most likely be wanting to communicate about it on their menus and signage.

Saving money on accommodation also means having more money to spare for supporting local amenities such as national parks, activity centres and other unique local experiences; you'll have a richer and more varied experience than you otherwise would have.

Don't allow your worry about green actions stop you from travelling to new places – visit anyway, ask your questions and try your hardest to put your own green actions in place. You may educate or inspire someone to follow in your footsteps, or even just get a hotel owner thinking about their responsibilities towards the environment. You may also learn from someone else, see a new green technology you've never heard of or find yourself inspired by local people. Policy makers in every country are making positive changes for a greener and less polluted world, so go and see what's out there.

Travel Stories: The Cherry on Top

She looked at us curiously as we digested the question she'd asked us. Tom and I looked at each other, feeling a bit like goldfish in a bowl, neither sure of how to answer the question. The seconds ticked on, and the enquiring woman repeated her question.

"Why have you come here?"

I smiled and decided to answer as concisely as possible. "Why not?"

"We just don't get tourists here." The woman replied in stilted but near-perfectly-pronounced English, "No-one thinks there is much here to see."

Slow and Sustainable Travel

I realised I needed to explain how we came to be sitting in Il Caffé in Castrop-Rauxel, in the Eastern Ruhr area of Germany. But my brain faltered when considering how I could explain our journey succinctly and effectively? How could I squash our life-altering decision to rent our house out, sell most of our possessions, start to housesit full time and travel the world whilst working remotely into a short sentence?

"We do housesitting. Have you heard of it?" is what I opted for in the end.

The woman and her family hadn't heard of it, and we conversed with them for a short while about what housesitting is and what it entails. There were a lot of "Ooh's" and "Aah's" from the German locals and finally, a nod of understanding from the woman who originally enquired as to our motives for being present in the café that day.

As I eagerly loaded another spoonful of one of the best desserts I've ever had into my mouth – light and soft waffles with sweet whipped cream which clashed deliciously with a homemade cherry compote – I pondered two things: the first was, "Why wouldn't everyone want to come here?", and the second was, "Am I perhaps the luckiest person in the world?"

Responsible Travel

Responsible travel is not only better for our world, it is also more interesting and memorable. Simon Reeve

Responsible travel includes being socially, culturally and politically sensitive to, and aware of, the place you are visiting. In the worst-case-scenario, tourists take no interest at all in the local culture and disrespect local traditions and customs. When we act in a lewd and disrespectful manner in our favourite holiday destinations, we have been labelled "Brits abroad." Some people seem to wear this slogan as a badge of honour – getting as drunk as they can on the plane, trashing their hotel rooms and leaving a trail of destruction in their wake. However, although we have this reputation, hopefully most of us don't act in this way and it's not too late to change this worldwide perception of us.

Being Culturally Sensitive

A good way to get started, is to educate yourself on your destination in advance, and order a good guidebook; Lonely Planet, Rough Guides and DK Eyewitness Guides are all good options. You can order pocketbook versions of these which are handy if you want to take them with you and have them on you whilst you explore. There is usually a section in the guidebook on any relevant political issues, cultural sensitivities and small

Responsible Travel

snippets of language for you to utilise. These sections of guidebooks are the first place I look; they are critical if you are going to really understand a place, adhere to social norms, and be respectful to the people that live there. Learning the language of a place, even if spoken in stilted pronunciation and with a terrible accent, is a great way to engage with local people. I do this everywhere I go, with "hello", "goodbye", "please" and "thank you" being top of my learn-list. My husband's top phrases to learn are "one pint please" and "cheers". Not only will learning a small part of the language give you more confidence as a traveller, it will allow the locals to see that you take an interest in their culture. They will often help you with the pronunciation until you get it right. Language opens doors to friendship and communication that we often keep closed by expecting the entire world to speak English.

One tip given by Chris Haslam is to read a book set in that location either before or during your trip. The book's narrative will be brought to life through your visit, and you may find yourself noticing more things about your surroundings than you otherwise would have. An example given was the travel memoir, *The Shadow of the Sun*, by Ryszard Kapuscinski about the author's travels through Africa.

It's also a good idea to check out information on gestures, and how to be respectful at cultural sites. Gestures are perceived differently around the world. For example, a thumbs up in America has positive connotations, meaning "good job", or "yes", while in Iran it is the equivalent of swearing at someone. In Malaysia, pointing at something with your index finger is considered rude, so people use multiple fingers to point, or don't point at all. Using your hand or fingers to beckon someone over to you would be acceptable in the UK, but in the Philippines it is very offensive and an arrestable offence. In Japan, people avoid making too much eye contact because it's considered disrespectful. In Greece, Bulgaria and Albania, head shakes are reversed so that a nod up and down means "no", and a shake from side to side means "yes". In some countries such as Egypt and China, burping after a meal is considered flattery and shows how much you enjoyed the meal while in countries such as the UK, this may be considered very rude. All of these differences can cause uncomfortable misunderstandings for the unwary traveller, ranging from mild confusion to being imprisoned in a foreign country. So, it's wise to get smart on local gestures and avoid making faux pas while you are there.

Another local custom to check, is whether it is customary or not to tip service staff. In the US, staff can't survive without their tips, so you must add them on. In the UK, you tip if you think your service has been good. In Australia and New Zealand tips are not expected, similar to Thailand, Vietnam and Cambodia where it is not expected but also not frowned upon. How to greet people is often different in each place; handshakes in the UK, kissing on the cheek in France, putting your hand on your heart in Malaysia and bowing in India. Public displays of affection are often frowned upon or banned in some Islamic countries and considered serious offences.

Visiting culturally important heritage sites is something that you are likely to do at some point on your travels. Who goes to Rome without seeing the Colosseum? Or to Alice Springs without going to see Uluru? Most of us are interested in the history, architecture and culture of these sacred places. Others may want to visit for more personal reasons such as family or religious connections. Whatever your reason for visiting, read up on the "do's" and "don'ts" before you go. Religious sites – such as churches in Italy – usually require you to cover your shoulders, and knees. If you don't have a means of covering up, the venue sometimes hand out plastic ponchos (not very eco), or refuse you entry altogether. As a result of unprepared tourists at such venues, there has been an increase in shawl-sellers at these locations to cater for the caught-off-guard travellers. Religious sites may also require you to take off your shoes, or require that quiet is kept throughout your visit. Others may be closed during prayer times, or only allow males, or females. So it's worth checking up on all of these points beforehand.

Responsible Travel

A word to the wise – research each heritage site before you visit it; just because a place is well-known or infamously linked to that destination doesn't mean it should be number one on your places to visit. Ask questions from your host, hotel staff, or any locals that you meet; you may find out about more unheard-of destinations that are not only more interesting to you but that could do with the support.

It is also worth doing a Google search for an update on the current affairs of any place you are about to visit – it's good to be informed about any potential political upheaval, protests, or other instabilities that might be taking place there so that you can be prepared. There may be places that are simply not safe to visit at the moment, and you can confirm this on the government foreign travel advice online. There may be mention of any ongoing problems in the media which you can actively research to get a more neutral viewpoint on them. It may be that there are no restrictions on travelling there and you feel the risks are not great. Or, it may be that it is just a small area of a country that you need to avoid. For example, the Darien Gap is a 10,000sq mile section of jungle on the Panamanian Columbian border in which there are no roads due to the swamp lands which makes overland crossing impossible. Crossing the gap is also a no-travel zone due to it hosting lawless drug runners, mercenaries and guerrillas. In other places, there may be certain historical political reasons why your visit to a place may cause an issue. For example, if you are a passport-holder of a nation that once imprisoned the native people, or of a religion that is currently in conflict with the locals, then you may find that the tensions in that place reverberate through the community in such a way that you would feel on edge if you visited now, or that it would make your trip less enjoyable. It's all a balancing act for you to navigate.

How to be Green in Someone Else's Home

If you think you are too small to be effective, you have never been in bed with a mosquito. African proverb

When we started on this epic adventure of travelling while living in other people's homes for months at a time, I never envisaged myself writing a book on the specifics of how to live your best green life on the road. Although I've always been a staunch advocate of living in the most environmentally friendly way, I was never a full-blown eco-warrior who applied those aspects to every facet of my living, breathing existence. Until recently. When I started living life on the road this time around in 2022, I found myself thinking more and more about the effect I was having on the planet. I had always considered my carbon footprint when physically travelling, but now new considerations, such as water usage, food miles, and pollution from cleaning products and bathroom products, cosied up to those original carbon concerns. I started to think about where everything I used came from, and where it was going. I spent hours changing up my use of disposables to reusables, from chemicals to naturals, from plastics to biodegradables. I researched places I wanted to visit in the areas we were staying, honing in on locations where projects were being conducted to rewild environments, build eco-centres, educate on regional wildlife, champion local seasonal produce or conduct green initiatives that were intriguing to me.

The choices I made every day now started to reflect my thinking. For example, when my deodorant was running out, I scoured the market to find a sustainable, natural and zero-waste option (check out www.wearewild.com). When I was buying Christmas presents, I looked for products with zero packaging, and bought fabric gift wrap made from recycled sari's produced by a fairtrade supplier. When I purchased coffee, I began to enquire as to where the coffee beans had come from. In all of these transactions I asked questions; just because something appears to be green or environmentally friendly doesn't mean it actually is. Beware of clever packaging and slogans. Ask the person you are buying it from. If they don't know where the money is going, or can't converse about the supplier they get their products from, then they probably don't do what they say on their green-labelled tin. It can be hard to find the truly green products among the many that are merely coated in "greenwash" marketing.

Now it's all well and good going around making your green choices and ensuring you speak to people in shops or restaurants when you are buying things, but you also need to take on the eco-lifestyle at home. It's one thing to offset your emissions (in any case a questionable concept), the most important thing is to reduce your carbon footprint in the first place. To do this, you must take a long hard look in that not-so-green tinted mirror and see which areas of your life are not adhering to your green-hued ethos. Are you a meat eater who buys all your meat from a large supermarket? Are you proud to support cafés that sell fresh local produce but at home you eat ready meals and freezer food without checking where it came from? Are you used to putting on the heating frequently but have never checked whether or not your home is properly insulated? Do you recycle most of the time, except when the container is too gross to clean out so you simply chuck it in the main landfill bin? Do you have a shopping addiction or simply have far too many clothes? We all have at least a few lifestyle habits that cater to speed and comfort over sustainability and the environment. The good news is that, once you spot these soul-sucking habits, you can eliminate them one by one. I'm not saying you can overnight blitz your way into a life of perfect shiny green living, but by welcoming in new thinking patters, doing some research, and making slow changes, you can be a somewhat eco individual very quickly.

Having rented out our own home to tenants in order to move from housesit to housesit, and having nowhere to go other than hotels or Airbnb's if we can't get a housesit for a certain period, leaving a gap in our full-time itinerary can be a daunting prospect. We often book housesits up to six months in advance, and it can be done further in advance than that. As I'm writing this (October 2022 by the way), there are already housesits available for next October on the app that we use. However, we do have to remind ourselves that now we are trying to be as green as possible, we need to consider our housesits more carefully. As mentioned in previous chapters, housesits often have a certain amount of automatic green credentials because they are off-grid, run by renewable energies, or harvesting their own water supplies. They may also grow their own vegetables or have chickens that supply eggs. Whatever green methods they use in their home, they will put these key features on their listing and then discuss them with you at length if you apply. They will need you to take on these ideals during your stay and will ensure that you understand the importance of things such as only flushing paper, pee and poo down a toilet that is connected to a septic tank, or how to compost kitchen and garden waste, or which water supply to use for what. Depending on the home, land, geographical location and local facilities, green routines and practices will likely vary slightly so if you're not sure on something, it's always best to ask the homeowner.

Let's start with something we all love to talk about – food. While you are staying in someone else's home, the owners may grow fruit or vegetables in the garden, in greenhouses, or even indoors (chilli plants thrive in warm environments and are often grown on windowsills). They will encourage you to eat any growing food that is in season and will go off before they're home. If you are caring for chickens or ducks who are laying, you will also be urged to eat any eggs they produce. In our current housesit, we've had two weeks of eating garden produce such as leeks, potatoes, tomatoes and eggs from the poultry. In Tom's words, we have been eating in food metres, not miles! If you grow your own vegetables and use a vehicle to travel from house to house, I'm sure the owners won't mind you bringing a few potted plants inside (mushrooms, chilli's, tomatoes etc. can be cultivated in pots and travel quite well).

If you can go completely plant based in your diet, then great. It's shown to be the best stuff to eat to reduce your carbon footprint even further; greenhouse gases released by livestock, farming machinery and soil disturbance are one of the largest contributors to global carbon emissions.

But a no-meat diet doesn't suit everyone, and if you can't go completely cold turkey (or no turkey), then try cutting out red meat or reducing it to one or two days per week. If you're going to buy meat, try to always buy free range, outdoor bred, and/ or organic. Most villages in the UK have a butcher who sells fresh meat sourced from local farms. Small independent butchers used to be more expensive to buy from than supermarkets, but due to the economic crisis it seems that the price gap is now smaller than ever. My husband will not eat an entirely plant-based diet and I recently went to the butchers to buy him some local meat. The cost of the chicken, pork and beef that I purchased was £11, and I used Tesco's online shopping calculator to work out that if I'd gone to their stores, I would have paid £10.20 for the same weight and types of meat. There is no longer the excuse of local butchers being too expensive. Another good thing about supporting local butchers is that you get a more personal experience; they can, for example, tell you what cuts of meat are best for certain recipes, or the best way to cook the meat you are buying. They have a wealth of knowledge that you can tap into and create a more meaningful experience from.

Buying food from local suppliers is a great way to cut down your food miles, reduce carbon emissions and support smaller independent businesses. Farmers markets are great places to find fresh seasonal vegetables and fruit, alongside other locally produced goodies whether it be alcohol, biscuits or honey.

The by-product of food is naturally going to be food waste. Obviously, we want to reduce food waste where possible so if you have leftovers, reheat them and use the next day or get inventive and make something new out of them. It's old fashioned and frankly quite dull to consider leftovers as boring, past their best or inedible. Unless something has gone off – sour to smell, visible mould or tastes off – then it is usually perfectly fine to eat. For anything that has gone off, or for fruit and vegetable peelings and other food waste, compost is the answer! Most households in the UK can get a free food waste bin from the local authority. The UK government have recently indicated that they will provide weekly food bin collections for every household by the end of 2023. This policy aims to encourage food composting and reduce the build-up of natural pests that result from composting such as smells and flies. Some homes we've stayed in have larger composting systems in the garden where all food waste goes into one compost bin and garden waste goes in another. Other homes have had multi-process composting systems whereby one food bin is kept in the house which when full is then emptied into a small food bin outside to start the break-down process, and then this is piled onto a compost heap near to the vegetable patch.

If you arrive at a housesit and they don't have a food bin or any composting system, don't think "Yippee I've got out of my boring food waste duties." Instead, think outside of the box; speak to neighbours about how they get rid of food waste, if you're in the area for long enough request a food bin from the council, or find a local recycling centre that accepts food waste. For your waste, the onus is on you, not the homeowner. Moreover, if you get a composting system in place, perhaps you can get them to change their habits!

How to be Green in Someone Else's Home

Recycling all your other used products is also of the utmost importance no matter where you are geographically. The UK has frequent recycling bin collections run by the local authority in most areas. The homeowner whose house you are looking after should let you know about the system; which coloured bins are for which items and what day the recycling goes out, where to place the bins and whether collection types vary each week. Every local authority in the UK runs these systems differently. In Gloucester where we are from, the big black bin is for general waste, whereas in Hampshire where we currently are, the general waste goes in the big green bin. Whoever it was in Hampshire council that thought of putting the big bad waste into the green bin gets a big thumbs down from me. The service may be run in a very organised fashion or conversely in a very disjointed and haphazard way. You may find that on some weeks the bin men simply don't turn up or are a bit scatty on times and dates. It's important to get to grips with the bin collection systems as soon as you can at a housesit to avoid unnecessary waste or recycling build up at the property. If you do find that you miss a week or that something isn't collected, you could make use of local recycling centres or the glass and plastic recycling points that can often be found by supermarkets or in town centres.

Many local recycling points also accept donations of second-hand clothes and shoes. When it comes to clothing, the best thing you can do once you've purchased something is use it for as long as you can; buy less and use each item longer. If an item gets a hole or a button comes off, mend it rather than throwing it away. If you can't mend it and the product is unusable then you may be able to find a project where textiles are collected to remake other products such as Recycle Now where clothing can be recycled via the local authority to make padding for chairs and car seats, cleaning cloths and industrial blankets. Some high street stores also ask for any old clothes (no matter the condition) to recycle the fabrics and may also offer you an incentive to do this such as a voucher or discount code.

The Housesitter's Guide to the Galaxy

Whether you are a fashionista or a throw-on-whatever-I-have-that-fits type, charity shops are the way forward. They are the new cool way to shop where you can find bargains and trendy items, and help the environment at the same time. Buying your clothes from charity shops used to be considered something that only people on low incomes did, but it has fast become one of the most in-style shopping habits in the UK. Buying second hand doesn't mean buying dirty or faded clothes – on the contrary – in charity shops I often find brand new items or items in fantastic condition, as well as designer or big-name brands. The shops themselves will usually wash items and will check them for holes or rips prior to resale. The sheer variety of clothing, shoes and accessories that can now be bought from charity shops is great. And it's not just clothes which these shops stock – the British Heart Foundation have specific stores for electrical goods and furniture; a great place to shop when you are looking to furnish your home. All electrical goods are PAT tested and date stamped to assure you they are in good working order. Books are also on sale in most charity shops regardless of the size – I've found brand new releases for £1 in some stores. As with any good recycling model, charity shops work both ways; don't just buy from them, but give them your second-hand items too.

When you are living in someone else's home you need to strike a good balance of looking after yourself and not taking advantage – the homeowner is paying the bills after all. I naturally feel guilty putting the heating on as I know how expensive it is, and I'm generally of the "put another jumper on" mindset. But sometimes it is just too darn cold; I'm sitting at a housesit wrapped in a blanket and shivering when the thought comes to mind that we should put the heating on. On checking the thermostat, it's 16 degrees Celsius and I realise I must be nearing hypothermia. I chuck the heating on and bask in the warm homeliness I feel (as well as my fingers and toes which had gone numb). Why do I feel guilty? I can only put it down to being a staunch stiff upper lip Brit who tries their best not to make a

How to be Green in Someone Else's Home

fuss. In this instance, putting the heating on was a fuss. I know, it makes no logical sense to freeze to death whilst caring for someone's home. I also realise that if I'm cold, the pets are cold, and that made my mind up instantly; I'd use the heating as and when needed. I am a sensible adult who doesn't take advantage of these things – but I realise that what I was actually concerned about, was someone thinking I was doing just that.

A measure of consideration about the amount of energy you use is important in any housesit – especially as you won't be paying the bills. I hear some of you doing a little skip and a jump at the thought of free unlimited heating or steaming hot baths every few hours, but get with the programme people! The energy required to heat or cool a home can be substantial, and you can't always be sure whether the energy comes from a renewable source or not. It may be worth asking the homeowner in advance – but either way, using more than you need is not a green way to live. So be conscious of your usage and reduce your heating and aircon usage wherever possible.

In a similar vein, you should be considerate and mindful of your water usage; don't leave the tap on while brushing your teeth, don't use the dishwasher unless completely full, don't have baths too often, and when showering, turn off the water when washing your body or hair. Remember to not water plants or grass if there is a water shortage or hosepipe ban in the area, and wear your clothes for as long as possible before washing them. These should be things you do wherever you are living, but they all deserve special consideration when you're living in someone else's property. As discussed before, you may want to apply to housesits that promote their use of natural water sources such as wells or streams, or sits where the homeowners have installed water tanks to catch rainfall that they use for the garden or for crops. They may even have systems where grey water – relatively clean waste water from showers, baths, sinks, washing machines, and other appliances – is used to flush toilets or irrigate gardens. If they don't have these systems in place, is there a way you could put some makeshift solutions in place for the duration of your stay? For example, are there watering cans or containers you could place outside to catch rainfall for watering indoor plants?

Cleaning and household products are usually provided by the homeowner for you to use during your stay. However, they may want to use a product that you prefer not to use whether it be because they are not biodegradable, are harsh on your skin, or because they produce harmful VOCs or other toxins (products that are harmful to you as well as to the environment). In general, cleaning products are one of the main areas in which we need to clean up our act (pun intended). A weekly average of £2.70 was spent on cleaning products in UK households in 2021, which shows just how much cleaning stuff (sprays, wipes, sponges) we go through. One of the most established eco-cleaning brands is Ecover; all their cleaning products are made from plant-based, biodegradable ingredients, their packaging is made from recycled plastics, and they encourage the buying of refills. They sell everything from laundry detergent to dishwasher tablets and toilet cleaner; sure, they're more expensive than the regular brands but most things that contribute to a greener and more sustainable environment require you to put in a bit of extra wonga. These days there are more and more eco-friendly cleaning brands emerging, and in any supermarket in the UK or Europe, you will usually find an eco-friendly version of any product you are looking for.

When you're considering your vehicle usage, consider walking, cycling or using public transport when exploring the area or taking pets outside. Usually if we are looking after dogs, we like to walk them on leads until we get to a safe park or forest where they can run around – but walking dogs on leads for anything but short distances can sometimes be problematic. We have looked after dogs before that are bad on the lead – pulling and straining – which can make getting around difficult or sometimes downright impossible. Being a petite woman, I do find that sometimes the dogs are taking me for a walk; just the other day I passed a man on a walk who said "Looks like you're being dragged along there." I tried to smile but grimaced a look that I hope conveyed, *thanks for that friendly yet sarcastic observation while I try with all my 110-pound-might to get these hounds under control.* In these circumstances, the dogs may be better behaved, and your life much easier, if you chuck them in the car and drive to the park. It's ok to do this when needed – safety needs to be the first priority when you're looking after other people's pets.

Wherever you are housesitting – whether it be in the UK or anywhere worldwide, you are more likely to be staying in places that you had never considered visiting before. And when exploring the surrounding area – be that a nearby city or local attraction such as a National Trust property – using public transport can add to the experience. While cities usually have good public-transport networks, busses in rural areas are more hit-and-miss. However, if there is a local attraction such as a stately home or scenic spot, there are sometimes shuttle services to villages or nearby towns, so look out for those by asking around in tourist venues or local shops. If you are very rural, and the attraction is a local waterfall or something similar, the walk might be part of the fun or you might consider hitching.

For slightly more distant day trips, consider trains. We were recently at a housesit in Hampshire and wanted to explore the nearby city of Portsmouth a bit more. We hopped on a train and were there in 25 minutes having produced less carbon emissions = win, having had no difficulties parking = win, no arguments in the car about the best route to get there = win, and the bonus that both of us could have a few alcoholic beverages = mega win.

Alternatively, in several housesits we've undertaken, the hosts have offered us their bikes to use during our stay; we've always much appreciated this and the offer firmly taken up. Travelling around on two wheels instead of four is another great nod to the green life and contributes exactly zero to your carbon emissions. It's also great exercise, is exhilarating, and allows you to see areas from a new angle. Unlike in places such as Germany or the Netherlands where fantastically practical, scenic, and safe cycle lanes have existed for many decades, the cycling infrastructure in the UK and Ireland still leaves a lot to be desired. In the UK, we have often been forced to dance the cycling tango of death with road users consistently trying to hit, honk or swear at us. However, good news is on the horizon and cycle paths, lanes and routes have been at the forefront of several councils' agendas in the last ten years and they have been putting funds into regeneration and improvement of cycleways on a scale never before seen in the UK.

The best, easiest, and most enjoyable way of reducing your carbon footprint while exploring local areas is simply by discovering them on foot. I love to walk and I think it's probably the only type of exercise that I can do consistently, for hours at a time, without getting bored. Yes ok, I may sneak in a couple of pre-planned coffee (and I can hear a chorus from those who know me of "and cake") stops amid my two-legged wandering routes. But given that I'm doing something good for my health, as well as for the planet, why not do something good for the local cafés and suppliers too! Seems that if I really want to do some good for the world, I'll grudgingly have that oat-milk cappuccino topped with organic dark vegan chocolate while I shlep around a gorgeous country park; what a cross to bear.

Digital Nomads, Homeworkers and Housesitting

Never get so busy making a living that you forget to make a life.
Dolly Parton

Housesitting is the perfect solution for anyone who doesn't need to be physically present in the office or in the workplace to earn a living. A digital nomad is someone who works remotely and has no fixed location; they move around travelling from place to place and pay for accommodation as they go. They can earn a living by working online so the only thing they rely on is a good internet connection. Digital nomads have been on the rise in the last decade or two since the world has become more reliant on technology and communications. Most digital type jobs can be done from anywhere and this suits people who like to travel.

Digital nomad (DN) visas have been around for a long time but are now on the rise and available in more countries than ever before. Just recently, Spain have brought out a new version open to non-EU citizens which gives them the chance to live and work in Spain for up to five years. The visa is for people who work remotely for companies based outside of Spain, and you have to prove this by showing a contract or proof of freelancing if self-employed. As with most digital nomad visas, there is an income threshold for which you have to prove that you can support yourself financially while you are in the country. For the Spanish

DN visa this is currently set at €28,000 per year or roughly €2350 per month. There are now digital nomad visas in countries all over the world – from Bermuda to Costa Rica, Portugal to Norway, Namibia to Bali.

A "homeworker" is slightly different – it's a term that came to be during the Covid-19 pandemic whereby people were required to stay at home, and so employers had to be flexible and evolve business policies to allow their employees to work effectively and efficiently outside the office. Although at the time, this was an enforced policy and lots of people struggled with the isolation, lack of interaction with colleagues, and sedentary lifestyle changes, homeworking is something that is now here to stay. Several people I know never went back to the office; their employers realised that they could get rid of the major overheads involved in running a physical office space and so they closed them down permanently.

This swing from office working to homeworking has resulted in a new contemporary way of life that is more accommodating to employees and more adaptable. In some ways it feels almost as though the working world has realigned itself towards the employee; considering their personal lives as well as their contractual working agreements – and having the potential to create a better equilibrium for the employee between the two. This flexibility suits a lot of people and gives the employee more scope to manage their own work-life balance. Generally, as long as they get their work done and are available for meetings and responsive to messages, employees are now given more freedom than ever before. They may be able to go to the gym, do their shopping, or walk their dog within working hours, saving them time and money if they were previously paying for doggie day care. Employees that now work from home also benefit from the lack of commute – saving them time that they can fill with more beneficial things – more sleep perhaps! The lack of commute also reduces their need to rely on a vehicle, cuts down their bill for fuel, and has a positive impact on the environment.

Digital Nomads, Homeworkers and Housesitting

The great news for both digital nomads and homeworkers is this – housesitting could provide the key to unlocking an even greater amount of freedom for you. Both types of remote worker would thrive if they were to marry their current working practices with housesitting – whether as a way of travelling the world or simply living rent free.

My husband and I both work remotely while housesitting, so the ability to work is something that we prioritise when we are moving around. Our income covers our expenses such food, petrol or travel to/from housesits, car insurance, activities and various other lifestyle costs. Tom began working remotely in July 2022 which gave us the ultimate freedom to move around and allowed me to quit my job and start a journey of writing that I'd dreamt of doing for years. Housesitting was a great chance for us to travel in a more meaningful and slow way while unlocking the door to financial freedom and the chance to actually start living.

Not only that, but working remotely from a housesit is easy peasy. Homeowners understand that a lot of people work remotely and are always more than happy to talk to us about their Wi-Fi connections and speeds. Make sure that this is not the first question you ask them, perhaps slot it in at the end of a video call to help them understand that their pet and home is a high priority for you. The housesit does need to work for both parties; it's a trust exchange in which you are giving of your time and effort to look after the homeowner's home and provide their pets with love and care, in exchange for a suitable place to live and work. If your bottom line is a roof over your head and a good Wi-Fi connection, then make sure you are clear about this and discuss it with the homeowner before agreeing to the housesit.

As well as checking they have a Wi-Fi connection, if you are worried about connectivity, you can also ask them to do a speed test and send you a picture of the results. This is not too much to ask – you are going to be looking after their most precious possessions, so it's only logical that you make clear what your requirements are.

If you are going to be housesitting in a country where power cuts are frequent, discuss this with the owner. Ask as many questions as you can think of such as: How often do they happen? How long do they usually last? Is there a generator? Does the homeowner have any advice for you for when this happens? Do they have a backup router, connection or internet dongle? Remember, there is no such thing as a stupid question, especially when it comes to your livelihood and peace of mind. It's not rude to ask these things. On the contrary, it shows that you are capable of foreseeing issues and want to minimise any problems for you and the homeowner while you are staying in their home.

Another thing that I'd recommend you do if you're going to embark on a remote working and housesitting adventure (trust me, it rocks) is to invest in your own back up device. Tom and I have purchased a dongle (this word always makes me laugh, yes I'm that immature). A Wi-Fi dongle or data card is in effect a small internet-connected hub that you can plug in – most frequently via the USB port, but wireless options are now becoming more available – to your laptop or device. This provides your laptop with internet in the same way that your phone uses the internet – via 3G, 4G and 5G networks. Usually, you can only use a dongle with one device at a time, but it depends on the type of dongle. Using the internet in this way means that you will be required to pay for your usage; so you'll need to set up a plan with the provider of the device (a bit like the way you'd pay for internet at home) and pay a monthly fee for a certain amount of data (e.g. £20 for 50GB).

You can also pay on an as-and-when-you-need-it basis. This is what we do – rather than paying a monthly fee and increasing our outgoings, we paid for the dongle outright which cost approximately £100. We then carry it with us and then when we need to use it we pay for a bundle of data (say, £10 for 5GB). The data is more expensive when purchased in this way, but we find that we don't actually need it often enough to pay for a monthly plan, so it works best for us and works out the cheaper option in the long run. The dongle we bought is the GlocalMe Duoturbo Mobile Wi-Fi 4G router, which is great for use globally as you can purchase data in over 140 countries. It doesn't require a contract or incur roaming fees, and it is small and lightweight.

But use of the dongle is always our last resort – if we can use the homeowner's Wi-Fi for our work then we will do so; they wouldn't usually disconnect their internet for the time they are away so they are paying for the internet either way. The internet connections that most people have in their homes is now pretty reliable and stable. Obviously, using their Wi-Fi is also free for us, and a lot easier than buying data and connecting one device at a time. However, having the dongle on us as we travel gives us peace of mind, and you can't put a price on that.

Housesitting Stories: Our Big Shot

We arrived at our first housesit feeling a little nervous but very excited. We'd been trusted by a lovely couple to look after their four dogs, cat and chickens and the setting couldn't have been better; a rural and cosy cottage in the Forest of Dean with incredible views, endless birdsong and a wood burner in the lounge. We wanted the sit to go well as we needed a good review to enable us to get more housesits and we really appreciated the fact that the homeowners had decided to let us look after their pets without any reviews and a relatively new profile. In short, this was our big opportunity.

On arrival we chatted with the homeowners for a good while – discussing pet needs, being shown where everything in the house was, shown the garden and outbuildings and made to feel at home. They gave us a really in-depth printed document too which had things such as emergency contact and vet contact details on it.

Tom unloaded his laptop and logged on as he was working that day, and I continued to chat to the homeowners as they got themselves ready for departure for their long weekend away. Just before they set off, they showed us that there was a path that ran the length of their property which the neighbour used to access their house. The path went past the front door and lounge window. They told us we'd see the neighbour and his dogs coming and going and not to worry or think there was an intruder. We nodded; no problem at all, we understood the situation.

"Oh and he goes out hunting sometimes. So basically, if you see a man walking past the window with a gun, don't worry it's just the neighbour!" one of the homeowners added on flippantly, both of them laughing and Tom and I joining in unconcerned – we weren't scared or worried by the situation and found it amusing.

That weekend passed by in a glorious mixture of cups of tea on the decking watching the birds, forest walks with the dogs, cosy evenings in front of the fire reading and several glasses of wine and good meals in local pubs.

Fast forward three months and fill in the gaps of a busy working and social life and several more housesits completed. One day, one of the homeowners from the Forest of Dean housesit we'd done in January messaged me to say they were going away again and they wondered if we would consider looking after their home and pets for another long weekend. Tom was going to be away that weekend, but I was around, so I proposed I took care of the pets on my own. The homeowners agreed and off I went, back to the haven of a cottage where we'd completed our first housesit, this time to enjoy the surroundings in Spring.

The entire sit went smoothly and I enjoyed being reunited with the pets and spending time in the peaceful environment that the home and location offered. On my first day there alone I did a long walk with the dogs, spent time reading in the garden, did some yoga and mindfulness exercises and then settled in for the evening with a bottle of wine and a crime documentary. Later in the evening, perhaps 10 or 11pm, the shadow of a figure walked past the window carrying ominous-looking paraphernalia on his back.

A spooked feeling crept over me, and whether it was the wine or the crime documentary I'd been watching, I suddenly felt scared. I told myself I was stupid – I hadn't seen anyone, and went to make myself a cup of tea. As it was brewing, it hit me, it was the neighbour of course!

The Therapeutic Benefits of Housesitting

Never underestimate the healing power of that friend who is furry with paws. Diana Loomis

We all know that we should spend more time outside in nature – it's good for us. But how much do we know about the power that nature has to heal us? This chapter will delve into the benefits of spending more time outside and around animals, both of which housesitting facilitates. Housesitting has given me the opportunity to spend more time outside than ever before in my (almost) thirty years on the planet. Spending time with animals and spending time in nature, often go hand in hand; not only am I spending more time with the pets, but I'm also spending more time in nature as I walk dogs, tend to cattle, or feed chickens. I may be caring for someone else's garden by weeding, mowing lawns, watering plants, checking greenhouses, or harvesting fruit or vegetables. Nature doesn't have to be a far-flung place of wilderness; nature can be a back garden, a local dog-walking field, or a paddock full of sheep.

There are many forms of therapy available in the modern world, but I find that nature is the most pure and simple form of therapy; and it's available for free. In 2018, the writer Stephen

Nett wrote about new research that shows the positive impacts of nature on physical and mental health. Citing a paper by Howard Frumkin of the University of Washington, Nett wrote that something as simple as hospital patients having a view of the natural landscape – trees – outside their window, meant that they healed faster and required less pain medication than those who had the view of a brick wall. A 2016 study in Australia showed that those who visited a park each week for as little as thirty minutes had lower blood pressure and better mental health than those who didn't; and this was simply a visit to a park – without even exercising.

In 2010, Qing Li, a researcher at Nippon Medical School, conducted some research that showed that when people walk through forest landscapes, they inhale phytoncides (airborne chemicals that plants give off to protect themselves from insects and help to fight disease) which increased their number of "natural killer" cells. These are white blood cells that support the immune system and help to combat infections and reduce inflammation, which in turn help to reduce the occurrence of heart disease, diabetes, and possibly even cancer. So these phytoncides benefit not only the trees themselves, but also the humans that walk through them!

Attention and concentration spans can also be improved by spending time in nature – as shown in a study by the University of Michigan where short-term memory was improved by up to 20% after a walk in natural surroundings as opposed to a walk through urban streets. So, if you are looking to boost your creativity, improve your effectiveness at work, or fight health conditions associated with memory loss, spending time in nature can be a great help.

With regards to mental health conditions, a 2022 study in the International Journal of Mental Health and Addiction, demonstrated that participants with anxiety experienced positive results and reduced symptoms after spending just fifteen minutes a day outside for nine days in a row. The study found that nature allows the body to decrease its stress levels and regulate hormones organically.

In 2020, individuals with bulimia nervosa were interviewed and asked about their experiences with their conditions and healing sources. Participants said that nature had helped them to reconnect with their bodies and feel calmer and more ordered. In the non-judgemental world of nature, the mindset of these individuals showed marked improvements.

Richard Louv, the author of *Last Child in the Woods*, writes, "Nature is not only nice to have, but it's a have-to-have for physical health and cognitive functioning." The leading mental health charity in the UK, Mind, has a dedicated page on their website identifying how nature can help with mental health. They say that "growing food or flowers, exercising outdoors, or being around animals" can "reduce feelings of stress and anger," "improve your confidence and self-esteem," "reduce loneliness," and "improve your mood."

Over the last couple of years, a new phenomenon has emerged across the world, seeing clubs formed, and books and articles written, encouraging everyone to give it a try – wild swimming. A fun and possibly crazy initiative created to give your day a bit of a boost, wild swimming also has several health benefits. A study by Charles University found that cold-water immersion can boost dopamine (also known as the "happy hormone") levels by 530% – thereby helping to relieve pain, improve wellbeing, and make us a whole lot happier! The same study found that wild swimming increases our metabolism, aids weight loss, and improves sleep quality. Other studies have corroborated these findings, demonstrating that wild swimming can reduce pain and inflammation, and that those who go wild swimming are more resistant to illnesses and infections due to an increase in white blood cells.

First discovered in Japan in the 1990s, the practice of *shinrin-yoku*, or "forest bathing," was shown to have huge benefits, and the

Japanese quickly embraced it as a form of ecotherapy. It has since spread across the world as a relied-upon form of therapy. Today, it is a popular phenomenon and you can book ecotherapy excursions with trained guides throughout the UK and overseas who will take you on meditative and restorative journeys.

So it's pretty clear from studies conducted all over the world that simply getting outdoors and into nature, and breathing in fresh air, is a great way to reduce the symptoms and prevalence of physical and mental illnesses. But what about being around animals? There are also a huge number of studies that show that being around animals and pets can also have a dramatic effect on our wellbeing.

In 2020, the Healthcare Counselling and Psychotherapy Journal produced a report that stated that animals can support our mental health and can actually assist in the treatment of certain conditions such as addiction and depression. Dogs in particular are shown to respond to the emotions of their human companions and can help to improve our mood dramatically. Animal-assisted therapy (AAT) involves interacting with animals as part of a patient's treatment plan. Dogs are used frequently as a form of AAT and the therapy has been proven to benefit adults with Alzheimer's and children with autism.

Welfare dogs have been taken into hospital wards in order to increase positivity and improve recovery in patients, and more recently, into office buildings to improve morale among staff. A study published in the *American Journal of Critical Care* in 2007 showed that visits from therapy dogs in hospitals improved cardiovascular health, lowered blood pressure, and lowered stress levels, in cardiology patients.

There is evidence that when in the presence of animals, humans produce the hormone oxytocin which increases bonding and communication while lowering levels of stress and anxiety. Oxytocin has also been shown to relieve pain such as headaches and cramps. A study in Japan in 2008 showed that even just eye contact between humans and dogs could increase oxytocin levels in humans.

In relation to addiction, one study involving 17 patients diagnosed with substance abuse showed that animal-assisted therapy improved everyday skills, and decreased levels of impulsiveness which allowed them to reduce their substance misuse.

Although animal-assisted therapy most commonly involves dogs, there are several studies that show that horses can also have positive impacts on the treatment of patients with both mental and physical health conditions. Research conducted in 2021 investigated the effects of Equine Assisted Therapy on the reduction of Post-Traumatic Stress Disorder (PTSD) – a disorder commonly experienced by military veterans. The therapy consisted of patients getting involved with all aspects of horse care including handling, grooming, mucking-out and riding. The study was overwhelmingly successful in reducing the PTSD symptoms of the group who all reported decreased levels of anxiety and loneliness.

A 2009 study in the Journal of Vascular and Interventional Neurology showed that cat ownership can also reduce the risk of death from heart attack and all other cardiovascular diseases – including strokes. Further studies on the healing power of cats show that their purr can be therapeutic for humans. The Fauna Communications Research Institute specialises in bioacoustics (sounds produced by living things) and has studied the frequency, pitch, loudness and duration of purrs in cats. It has found that a cat's purr can be medically beneficial when it is in the range of 20-140Hz.; it can assist with pain relief, wound and bone healing, and muscle repair, and can reduce swelling and improve joint mobility.

A study at the State University of New York found that cat owners are more likely to have lower blood pressure, reduced heart rates and lower levels of anxiety. It has also been shown in several studies that simply stroking a cat can lower your blood pressure – incredible right?

From all this research, it seems overwhelmingly clear that nature really can heal us. It has been proven time and time again to have incredibly positive impacts on numerous physical and mental health conditions. And you don't have to have a diagnosed condition to be able to benefit from nature. The fact is that simply living in the modern world is enough to create stress in our lives. The digital age is complex and overwhelming. A world driven by consumerism can leave you feeling guilty, empty, or lacking. Environmental or political concerns might cause anxiety or depression. You may feel you don't identify with other people in today's social media world. You may feel lonely due to less in-person interactions. The simple relentless business of modern life may leave you exhausted or feeling trapped. All of these feelings are valid and so spending more time in nature or around animals can help all of us to improve mood and outlook. Apart from the huge array of benefits that owning a pet provides, looking after pets also has the potential to increase your social interaction; they get you out of the house – they may need exercising, stables/pens clearing out, or simply require some company! Pets can also help to fulfil emotional needs such as love, security, comfort and companionship.

I've always been a lover of animals and as soon as we bought our first house, I rescued a fifteen-year-old cat named Selma who had been taken in by a local cat charity after her owner had passed away. I'm a believer of the idea that "a house isn't a home without a pet." I have a longing to have companionship from animals wherever I am. We had to have Selma put to sleep in 2022 when she was nearly eighteen – but we knew that she had really enjoyed her retirement with us. Being around Selma made me feel calm, connected and comforted. She gave the house life. When she was gone, the house felt empty and I felt sad whenever I looked around and couldn't see her. I considered getting another cat, but then Tom got a remote job and we wondered whether 2022 was the year for us to finally live our nomadic life. I have always bonded with the pets on a sit very quickly and have felt refreshed from spending time with a variety of different animals. Once Selma had gone, housesitting was my way back into quality time with pets – I got to cuddle them, exercise them, clean them, feed them and look after them. It was the perfect solution.

So housesitting is not just a great way to travel the world for free; housesitting can provide you with a form of therapy. It can provide you with the tools to improve your physical and mental health by giving you space and time to breathe and make plans, allowing you to decide what you want from life, and put a plan into action that works for you. Housesitting can unshackle you from the chains of societal expectations, contemporary living, fast fashion and social media. Housesitting can be short term or long term, a temporary period in your life or a permanent way to live. It can be full of a variety of different animals, or you can specifically look after just one type of pet if that's what you prefer. What I'm saying is that housesitting can be its own form of therapy.

After housesitting for over a year now, I have come closer to nature than ever before. Spending more time with animals and being outdoors has improved my mental and physical health. I am fitter and have a more positive mindset than ever before. Since beginning this journey, I have hiked, gardened, and tried wild swimming, forest bathing, and foraging – all of which have made me feel rejuvenated and connected, and none of which I would have had the opportunity or time to try if I was still working a 40-50-hour week.

Making the decision to housesit has allowed me to take control of my life and do something different with it. It has been more freeing and liberating than I'd ever thought possible, and it has allowed me freedom without living a full-scale nomadic life. I'm still very much in touch with the modern world but I live on my own terms. Housesitting has reignited my passion, my curiosity, my wonder, and awe. I have been able to find – no, trailblaze – my own path, create a work-life balance, travel as much as I want to, and be the boss of my own life. Go on, try it out, I promise you will feel the benefits.

A Note for the Homeowner

We must have infinite faith in each other. Henry David Thoreau

This book has been written primarily from the viewpoint of the housesitter because that's the area that I have experience in. Regardless of this, I'm acutely aware of how integral the homeowner is to the entire process – without whom there would be no housesitting! They sign up to the websites discussed earlier, and pay an annual subscription in the same way that the housesitter does. This fee allows them to search for and contact housesitters, advertise the dates they need their home and pets looked after, and create a profile to describe their home, their pets and the responsibilities that the housesitter will need to take on during their stay.

Being a "pet parent" – which is what one of the websites, Trusted Housesitters, refers to homeowners as – seems to me to involve an even bigger leap of faith than that of the housesitters. "Pet parents" are not only trusting you with their home, the valuables and personal possessions within their home, and their innermost sanctuary and shelter, but they are also trusting you to look after their pets. And let's face it, pets are family. Pets are like children to most people which is why they are often referred to as "fur babies." This is a big deal. Not only are they trusting the housesitter not to rifle through their knicker drawer or steal any possessions, they are literally handing their babies over to strangers.

When I consider the importance of the task, it blows my mind. Of course, Tom and I always try to get to know the homeowners as well as we can before the sit begins – this may include video calls, messages, meeting in person, having cups of tea, going for dinner, generally having long chats. In this way, the homeowner gets to know us better and can hopefully relax a bit about their pet and home being in safe hands. But I still admire what seems like an incredible leap of faith for homeowners. So, while I spent time pondering the role of the homeowner in the housesitting process, I decided that the best way to understand their point of view would be to ask them. I contacted a few of the people we've done housesits for and asked them a series of questions about the homeowner side of the process. I asked all of them the same questions such as: Would they recommend it to other homeowners? What had their experiences been like? What characteristics do they look for in housesitters? How do they determine if a sitter is trustworthy? I also asked some questions around using housesitting to encourage greener and more sustainable travel.

Housesitting from the homeowner's perspective:

"Absolutely I would recommend using housesitters. Even if we only had houseplants we'd look for sitters."

The responses were very positive; none of them reported a bad experience using housesitters and all of them said they would recommend using housesitters to others. Only one homeowner said they had pulled out of a housesit due to concerns over the sitter, but even this experience was put in a positive light and shows just how important the initial conversation or meeting between the homeowner and the housesitter is; it gives both parties the opportunity to get to know each other and decide whether they are the right person for the task.

A Note for the Homeowner

"We backed out of a sit as someone was giving off overbearing vibes – we knew that our pets wouldn't cope with that."

When it came to the subject of characteristics that homeowners look for in housesitters, the main points that came up repeatedly were: sitters who are animal lovers, sitters who demonstrate reliability, honesty and respect, and sitters who have experience or good reviews. Regarding trustworthiness, one homeowner said that they rely on their intuition, using both the wisdom of their age and experience, and also of their gut. This ties in with another homeowner who said they often go on instinct.

"We both rely on the wisdom of age and the wisdom from one's gut about whether someone is trustworthy. A few excellent reviews go a long way to completing that picture."

Further responses showed that communication prior to the beginning of the housesit is not just important but crucial to the process, and allows the homeowner time to gauge their gut feelings properly. All homeowners said that they like to talk to their housesitter in person or by video call before the sit begins so that they can get to know them. If the sitter gets on well with the pets and the homeowner can see this in person beforehand, then that will go a long way to putting the homeowner's mind at ease. Conversely if the sitter arrives and the homeowner doesn't feel they are the right fit for their pets or home, then they still have the chance to turn them down. Likewise for the sitter, if you arrive and meet the pets who are not quite as well behaved as you'd like, or have very demanding needs, it's not too late to say that it's not quite right for you. If geography means that meeting beforehand is impossible, then video calls are also a great way to check out a sitter's personality, and give each party the opportunity to ask questions and check expectations.

"We were able to meet Jess and Tom at our home before our trip and talk them through everything and of course, introduce them to the animals. This was of great comfort to me as you can tell so much from a person when you meet them and I was instantly put at ease."

One homeowner said that they appreciated a sitter asking them specific things before the sit – such as how much they wanted to be contacted while they were away. This is a good example of things to discuss in advance. You generally don't want to be bothering a homeowner more than once a day if they are on holiday. However, if there are issues with the pets or the home, then you need to be confident that you will be able to contact them immediately. I usually send pictures of the pets to the homeowner maybe once every few days, but I let the homeowner guide the conversation; if they message me frequently, I return with more messages and more photos. If they don't message me at all, I keep updates short and less frequent; in other words, play it by ear.

With regards to whether they'd done housesitting themselves, only one homeowner said that they also did housesitting, and commented that "I have often thought Trusted Housesitters is like Airbnb but with pets!" This shows the freedom that housesitting can provide you with, and if you're set on visiting a certain area, then you can choose to only apply for housesits in that area. You obviously have more responsibility than a regular Airbnb guest, but if you are an animal lover this is simply an added bonus rather than a chore; if anything, the company I get from pets is very much appreciated and sought after. And the other big positive about the process is that it is virtually free. So, it's like Airbnb with pets AND without any costs ... Still on the fence?

When asking homeowners about their thoughts on housesitting and its potential to promote greener travel, one respondent said that housesitting could hugely reduce the need for international travel, suggesting that the process could "encourage a staycation-exchange trend." Staycations increased in popularity during the pandemic when travelling abroad was difficult, and if housesitting could also encourage people to holiday closer to home, then we could prolong the positive green effects that the reduction in travel had during that time.

A Note for the Homeowner

All the homeowners I spoke to were keen on the move towards greener, sustainable travel. One homeowner commented that "housesitting gives people the chance to travel and explore the world in a fairly inexpensive way" and "it is a great way to experience other people's cultures, values and home comforts." Learning about, understanding, and respecting other people's cultures and values all around the world, is something that I strive to adhere to wherever I am housesitting. The fact that housesitting is inexpensive is an important factor in it being conducive to long-term and sustainable travel. It allows eco-friendly travellers like myself to spread the wealth a bit further within the communities that we're staying in. It enables the housesitter to spend a bit more on organic, local produce, attending local events, and generally getting more immersed in the community.

One homeowner commented that ideally all housesits would have "solar power or renewable energy, water from a spring, and an ability to recycle waste material without relying on any of the utility companies." Although most properties are a long way from ticking all these boxes, there are some out there that do. We have done housesits in homes within the UK whose water comes from a well on their land and whose electricity is completely solar powered. Some homes on the app that we use are off-grid completely, grow their own fruit and vegetables, have composting toilets and limited power supply. These homeowners will need housesitters who are respectful of these eco initiatives and will abide by any household rules they have in place to sustain them.

When discussing with homeowners any other positives they get from using housesitters, one respondent said that a huge bonus for them is that it allows their pets to stay at home while they are away. Another owner said that they have had such good experiences with housesitters that they don't even think about kennels or catteries when they plan a break away; getting housesitters now just forms an integral part of their trip-planning.

"The wonderful thing about it is that your pets get to stay in the comfort of their own home and have lots of attention (probably more than usual) while their owners are away."

The responses I received from homeowners were overwhelmingly positive, and though these are just a small handful of homeowners, and their length of experience with housesitters varies, their encounters with housesitters have all been fantastic. Several homeowners that I spoke with said that they had never thought of using housesitting for long-term travel but thought it would be a wonderful way to travel. One commented they wished they'd had the opportunity to do this when they were younger.

"What a fabulous way to be able to travel the world."

As you can see from my discussions with homeowners there are many positives to be had from this process for the homeowners as well as for the housesitters. I imagine that homeowners also gain some satisfaction from knowing that they are providing housesitters with a unique experience – with comfortable accommodation, heating or air conditioning, water, and services such as internet and TV. Most people have put a lot of love and care into their homes and are very proud of them; all the homes we've looked after have been thoughtfully decorated, inviting, cosy, and warm.

The homeowner is providing the housesitter with security and a home-from-home albeit for a short period of time. Some housesitters may have their own home that they are leaving vacant while they do the sit, but others don't have this luxury – some may be between properties at the time of the sit or have taken a leap of faith (like us) and have rented theirs out. Whatever their circumstances, the homeowner is providing them with the most basic of needs. This is no small thing, and homeowners who take part in the housesitting process should be proud that they are inviting people – be they nomads, travellers or holidaymakers – from all over the world to use their

A Note for the Homeowner

home as a base for a while, and enabling them to interact with their pets and explore the local area. You are not only helping out these humans, you are also supporting and bolstering local businesses as sitters will inevitably dine out, buy local produce and visit local attractions. Cheers to you, homeowner, you rock!

Freedom

A nomad I will remain for life, in love with distant and unchartered places. Isabelle Eberhardt

The main reason that we absolutely love our fulltime housesitting lifestyle is the freedom that it provides us with. Housesitting can help set you free from the chains of everyday life, reduce the amount you pay on bills, and smash the "getting on the mortgage ladder" idea by providing an alternative means of long-term accommodation for free. It can allow you to rent out any property that you do have which effectively means that someone else pays your mortgage. All of these things can help to reduce any money worries you may have in a world where consumerism is itself consuming us, and turning buying and owning into a competition between colleagues and peers.

Fulltime housesitting allows you to step off the wheel, leave the rat-race, and press pause on conventional life. It gives you time to refocus your priorities, get in touch with your own "life force", and figure out what you really want from your life. That common and overused saying, "You only live once" is so true; and if we only live once, why not live a bit differently? Why not rip up the rule book and write your own rules?

The possibilities that housesitting presents you with are endless – free holidays, free fulltime travel, a change in career, a change in lifestyle and it all starts from a change in mindset. Do you really want to spend the rest of your life working 40(+) hours in a job that you don't really enjoy or has no real long-term positive impact? Do you want to spend endless hours of your life commuting, or buying the pointless "stuff" that social media tells you is the next big thing?

Housesitting has allowed us to shed our consumer skins, to rid ourselves of stuff that we simply didn't need, and to live life on our own terms. You can do this too and all you need to start your own journey is the right outlook and determination. We all have a limited time on earth – allow housesitting to unbolt you from conventional life. Hell, who needs conventionalism anyway? Be bold, be bright, be true to yourself.

Location freedom is another huge benefit of housesitting. You get to decide on the areas you'd like to travel to, explore, or stay in on a longer-term basis. Every day can be different and exciting. You can escape the monotony that is normal life and choose to be free. Embracing this lifestyle is not always a walk in the park, it's not easy and it's certainly not for everyone. But if travel is calling you and conventional life is crushing you, housesitting could be the answer to your prayers.

Embrace yourself, embrace housesitting, embrace freedom.

The Top 10 Benefits of Housesitting

Do not go where the path may lead. Go instead where there is no path and leave a trail. Ralph Waldo Emerson

1. Travel

Without a doubt the biggest benefit for me, and the reason we initially set out on our housesitting journey, was to travel. It doesn't need to be abroad or somewhere off the beaten-track; we're interested in seeing all the areas of the world. Housesitting enables us to travel for longer periods of time, at a much slower pace, and visit unique locations that we wouldn't otherwise have thought of visiting. Through this lifestyle, we also meet people we would otherwise never have met – some of them fleeting, some lengthy, but always meaningful.

2. Financial freedom

With no utility bills to pay, no rent or mortgage costs and being able to work on the move, we've actually started to save money while housesitting; much more than we were saving at home. With the housesits providing us with free accommodation (minus the yearly membership fee), we have experienced a financial freedom that we've never felt before. It's meant that we can go for lunch, visit country parks, or buy souvenirs, whenever we feel like it.

3. Environmental impact

Staying for so much longer in each place, means it's easier to forego air travel and take slower forms of transport such as sea or rail instead. Staying for longer in a place, means more opportunity to buy local and support local green initiatives or conservation projects.

4. Cultural Impact

Travelling more slowly via housesitting also provides greater opportunity to get to know a place and its people. Unlike staying in most hotels, staying in people's home means that we are transported straight into local neighbourhoods. This gives us a great opportunity to mix with local people. Learning some of the local language, researching gestures, and generally being respectful of local cultures can help us to communicate and have more culturally rich exchanges. Do things like visit the pub, go to a gym class, attend a church service – but most importantly, speak to the people you see around. And because we are often staying in places that aren't necessarily used to receiving tourists, we can help to boost the local economies by buying local and supporting local businesses and visitor attractions.

5. Improved health and wellbeing

It's a fact that living your life the way you've always wanted to is going to make you feel great. The "slow travel" that housesitting has enabled, has allowed me to increase the amount of fresh home-grown food that I eat and increase the amount of exercise I do by walking dogs and joining local gym classes. It has allowed me time to just "be" in nature and has reduced the amount of stress in my life. Housesitting has helped me to make positive choices each day and to ensure that I keep my health and wellbeing in check – in a way that I never had time for in my previous hectic routine.

6. Perks

Low on the list for me and not something I actively look for when searching for housesits, but a benefit nonetheless – perks! As discussed, some housesits – through various different agencies and websites – can be paid work which is undoubtedly a big advantage if you need more income while you move around. Other perks that crop up in both paid and unpaid housesits can include the use of the homeowners vehicles, food in the house being left for you (make sure you check before you eat it, or replace what you eat if no agreement has been made), or use of homegrown produce such as homegrown vegetables, fruit, berries or eggs. Homeowners may also leave you membership cards with which you can visit National Trust properties, or English Heritage sides – allowing you to park in and enter places for free.

7. Career

If you have a job that you can do while on the move, then travelling in this way means you don't have to quit; you can have the best of both worlds. You can have your cake and eat it! The only thing you need to watch out for in very rural or off-grid sits is whether they have good internet access. Career-wise, housesitting can also give you the time, space and financial security to quit that soul sucking (or simply too static) job and try something you've always wanted to do. Look at me, I'm writing a book, something I've thought about doing since I was a teenager. If you've got a hidden passion you want to try and turn into a career, give it a go while you housesit!

8. Time to work on yourself

One of the biggest positives I have gotten out of housesitting so far is having more time to work on myself. I've had the time to join local exercise classes, attend local art classes, go to community meetings of interest, and have had more time to read the books I've always wanted to read. Volunteering, trying out different religions, and working on new creative skills have all been richly rewarding and have provided me with new perspectives on life. I can now spend time writing (fiction and

The Top 10 Benefits of Housesitting

non-fiction) and researching ideals that align with my own. Time is a gift and I feel that housesitting has gifted me more time than I'd ever dreamed of having.

9. The opportunity to live like a local

A very enjoyable part of housesitting is that you get to live in the area like a local – especially when you do as we do and look for longer housesits. We find that we have enough time to find our "favourite" pub/café/park/dog walk in the area. We spend long enough in a place to know the quickest walking route or the most scenic way to drive somewhere. We try out public transport, visit local shops and read the community notice boards with interest. Volunteering has been a great way to make friends with locals very quickly. While in Oxfordshire, I volunteered at Helen & Douglas House, a charity shop in Thame, and met some wonderfully friendly and inspiring women – I made some great friends there and hope to see them again when back in the area.

10. Pets

Last but definitely not least, the big one, the winner, the all-time top benefit you can get from housesitting is undoubtedly, *drum roll please*… pets. As a massive animal lover, the biggest draw of travelling in this way is that we get to look after a wide variety of animals. Having lived in our own home for a few years, we felt the house was empty without a pet (we did have a cat that had to be put down last year – miss you Selma) to fill the void; dogs were off the table as we worked such long hours and odd shifts. As travel has always been our main ambition and it's difficult to travel with your own pet, house and pet sitting provide a fantastic solution. It's the perfect combination. Looking after animals is like therapy for me (a free version with no one to talk back and tell you actually yes, you are mad), whether it be cuddling cats, walking dogs, feeding chickens, chatting to guinea pigs. Whatever the animal, I'm your gal. I've never been scared by any breed of any living thing (bar the odd human) and have been called an animal whisperer on multiple occasions. The only downside to this way of living that I have felt frequently, is the heartbreak that comes when leaving a housesit and it's pets. I form bonds quickly, so when I spend a month looking after a pet and it climbs into my heart, it doesn't just fall back out when I leave. I spend hours thinking about the pets I've looked after, wondering what they are doing and whether they miss me like a lovesick teenager. I often message homeowners a week or two after I've left to see how the pets are doing; they don't mind. I miss all of the pets we've looked after on this journey so far!

FAQs

The journey of a thousand miles begins with a single step. Lao Tzu

We've been doing the whole long-term housesitting thing for a while now, and as you can imagine we meet a lot of people on our travels around the world. Lots of people we've met, along with family and friends at home have asked us questions about housesitting that I'm sure a lot of you reading this will identify with. Some of them are things that had never crossed my mind while other are things I've spent a lot of time thinking about and get asked frequently. I'll outline and answer some of them below; you may find the answers aren't quite what you expected!

- Is it weird sleeping in someone else's bed?

A question one of my closest friends asked me when she came to visit me at a housesit in the UK, and something I'd never really given much thought to. As soon as she asked me, I laughed but realised it was a very valid question and something that many people may find odd or uncomfortable. Obviously, it all depends on the housesit; sometimes we are staying in a place with one bedroom which means that we have to stay in the homeowner's bedroom. At other times we may be staying in a bigger property and be given a guest room. It doesn't matter too much to me as long as the bed is comfortable and there is enough space to put our backpacks and unpack our stuff. If you do find this concept weird, try to imagine it like a hotel or hostel; thousands of other people have stayed in that room and bed, so as long as the space has been cleaned and the bed stripped and re-made, hopefully you can forget that you're technically sleeping in someone else's bed.

- Don't you get bored of packing/unpacking?

Well this one's a doozy. Yes, of course we do! The task of packing and unpacking can get boring. However, it's a necessary evil for anyone who travels long-term and isn't really a high price to pay to live the life we live. I tend to do my unpacking in one foul swoop if the space allows, and if owners have kindly left cupboard or drawer-space free, that really helps. Packing takes me a little more time and I tend to do it in stages; setting aside outfits for the last few days of the sit, and then packing up stuff I know I won't need before we leave. When it comes to food, we try to use everything up within the last few days. If there's food left over, we either take it with us in collapsible containers, or leave it for the homeowner (clearly stating when it was opened etc) or making a meal out of it for their return.

- What's the quirkiest pet you've ever looked after?

This is always a difficult one to answer. We've looked after ferrets before which were interesting and inquisitive creatures, but very stinky! Over Christmas 2022 we looked after a double yellow-headed African parrot. Neither of us had much (or any) experience in aviculture, and although I have long appreciated birds and their part in nature, to say I was nervous was an understatement. The homeowners would be gone for over a month and the parrot was used to socialising and coming out of the cage. We were warned, however, that if the parrot didn't like us, we'd soon know about it as she'd refuse to come out and possibly peck at us with her razor sharp - capable of shredding human flesh - beak. Great, we thought, we're going to end up covered in plasters. But the parrot, although shy at first, eventually trusted me enough to come out of the cage, progressing day by day until she would sit on my shoulder and we'd have a little sing along, whistling harmoniously (at least we thought so, I think Tom disagreed). She loved a head rub and came to grow very fond of me. It goes to show – if you're an animal lover, you can bond with most species!

- Do you miss the pets?

Another easy answer for me, big fat yes. I think Tom's answer would be that he misses some of them – perhaps the more well-behaved ones. Being a huge animal lover and most content whilst in the company of animas and pets, this is one of the hardest parts of the process for me. Housesitting goes hand in hand with looking after pets, and I bond with all pets very quickly. It's one of the reasons housesitting works so well for us – I simply adore the part where we look after animals. But although it can be heart-wrenching, whenever I feel the absence of a particular pet-friend, it reminds me that I'm good at this; reminds me that I'm good at housesitting and that I'm human and have been touched by nature and how wonderful it all is. That may sound like a load of old tosh, but it's the truest way for me to answer this question.

- Do you miss home? family? friends?

Another fairly easy but very common thing we get asked is whether we miss home and our family and friends. Yes, we miss them a huge amount. Yes, we think about our lovely little house and the warmth and safety we felt while living there. But in giving up our home, allowing others to take care of it, and leaving our hometown, we have begun a journey in which every day is different. We see places we'd never have travelled to, we meet people we'd never have met, we wake up with fresh and curious eyes every day, seeking out adventures, and experiences, and life. We feel exhilarated by the fact of just living. We often feel sad that we're missing things happening at home, that we aren't there enough for people, or simply that we can't give our mums a hug.

We miss our friends so much. I would say that the hardest part of this lifestyle for me is the loneliness. It can be difficult to make connections with others when we're only in each place for around a month. We have each other and that's a huge bonus, but sometimes we crave the company of others our age, of our friends back home and our families who know our background and stories. It can be difficult to have relaxed and easy-going interactions when we have to introduce ourselves and explain who we are, and what we're doing, and the rest of that gumpf. It's one thing that I've thought about at length – finding new ways to connect with others long-term such as online book clubs, writing forums and courses, and putting more effort into facetiming and speaking to family and friends at home.

- Has a pet ever died whilst you were looking after it?

No, thank goodness. It is something that crosses our mind now and then when we're looking after a particularly old or frail pet. We have had to look after pets with cones on, pets requiring lots of medication, dogs who have ripped open their stomachs on barbed-wire fences, finding and removing embedded tics in pets, and one very poorly chicken who we thought wouldn't last until the owners returned (she did!). It's something that inevitably happens now and then when people are looking after pets and housesitting. If the pet is older, the owner is probably aware that there is a chance it may happen while they are away – especially if the housesit is a long term one. If you are worried about this before doing a housesit, talk to the homeowner; find out where their vet is located, make a plan on how you would get there and keep the vet's details on your phone so they aren't difficult to find in an emergency. You can ask the owner beforehand if the pet has any medical issues that you need to be aware of – this may get them talking about emergency scenarios too. All you can do is be ready, and let nature take its course. If a pet does become unwell while in your care, immediately take them to the vets and seek advice. If you believe a pet will not last until their owner returns, let the owner know and seek their advice too. Stay in

FAQs

frequent communication with them during a time like this. Take care of their pet as if it was your own, and you will have done your very best during a very difficult time.

- What countries have you visited so far while housesitting?

Lately, our housesits have been in the UK, but we've done housesits in Germany, and have housesits planned for Norway, Spain and Kenya this year. The website we use, Trusted Housesitters, is global and there are sits available all over the world – from Los Angeles to Albania – so the future beckons!

- Wait, so you pay no bills, no rent, nothing?

You've got it. Currently our only major outgoings are food shopping, transport costs, phone bills and insurance (home and travel) and any activities we do e.g. quad biking in the Cairngorms (something we've done while on our housesitting journey).

- What is the website you use?

Trusted Housesitters. Check out the info earlier on in the book.

- How do I sign up?!

It's a question we get asked all the time. It takes a few minutes to sign up and a bit longer to create your profile, but then you're free to find out what housesitting could offer you and how it could change your life for the better.

The Nomadic Dictionary

Is freedom anything else than the right to live as we wish? Nothing else.
Epictetus

Beautiful words to inspire and resonate

Words are created to describe, explain and instruct. They are required to associate one thing with another. They are fashioned from trends and shaped by society and our everyday interactions. Some words have ancient roots in languages such as Latin or Greek while others have been newly created – becoming formalized from modern slang and taking shape from things such as street talk or music lyrics. There are no two ways around it; we need words to communicate. Words are used to inspire nations and educate children. They can be used to build people up or tear them down. They are one of the most powerful weapons in our arsenal – they can inflict pain or bring about peace. They can stimulate, motivate and encourage. Words are the backbone on which society is built.

Since I was a little girl, words have comforted me. I was an avid reader from a young age, loving the fact that I could open a book and enter a different world. Authors painted such vivid descriptions that I'd build cities in my mind, walk through jungles in my dreams, swim across oceans with whales, and swoop through the clouds with the birds. Since then, building upon these imaginative excursions, I also began enjoying non-fiction books. I learnt about great people in history, about wars and battles won and lost, I read stories of courage and hope and bravery, I read old books and new books across the range of genres – albeit with a soft spot for crime fiction, of course! Agatha Christie was the heroin of my teen years; I was attracted by mystery and having to figure things out, and by the idea that justice would come to all villains in the end. It was later, in my twenties, that I began reading about the adventures of those who had explored far-flung places, embarked on great expeditions, or who had devoted their lives to travel.

As a result of these readings, I've come across words that have motivated and encouraged me. These words have shown me that I'm not alone; that there are others out there who feel as I do, who want adventure, want to explore, want to witness the world's different cultures and languages, and who want to stand on as many different points of the atlas as possible and drink it all in.

Here are some of these words. I hope they inspire and resonate with you too.

Dérive [deh-ree-veh] – to move around or drift at leisure to no place in particular. French in origin and translated to mean "drifting", *dérive* is a way of moving through a city or a location – wandering aimlessly without direction or a destination in mind.

Eleutheromania [ell-loo-th-err-oh-may-nee-ah] – a great desire or obsession with obtaining and keeping freedom, a compulsive need for travel. A word with origins in ancient Greek mythology; *Eleutherios* meaning "liberator" was a label given to Dionysus, the God of wine and excess, who was known to be able to liberate people from their inhibitions.

Fernweh [Fown-vee] – this refers to a longing for distant places, a longing for new places, and a deep desire, or ache, for travel. German in origin, this word combines the words *"fern"* meaning distance and "*weh*" meaning pain or sickness. It is the opposite of the word Heimweh which describes homesickness.

Flâneuse [Fluh-noose] fem. / Flâneur [Fluh-nuor] masc. Someone who strolls or saunters around – not doing anything in particular but observing people and society. An urban explorer and person of leisure. This word has its origins in 19th century France; the French poet Charles Baudelaire said that the modern artist needed to become "a botanist of the sidewalk" (to study people like flowers) as it would enable him to understand and accurately portray a city.

Hodophile [Hoh-doe-file] – one who loves to travel. This word comes from the Ancient Greek word "*ὀδός*", pronounced "*hodós*" meaning "way", "passage" or "travel". The suffix "phile" means one who likes or enjoys a particular thing and translates as loving.

Livsnjutare [Lifs-nu-ta-ra] – a person who loves life deeply and lives it to the extreme. Swedish in origin, this word translates as an "enjoyer of life". It is used to describe someone who takes every opportunity to live life to the fullest.

Nefelibata [Ne-fe-li-ba-ta] – a person who lives in a cloud of their own dreams and does not conform to the rules of society. A person who follows their own path. This Portuguese word translates as "one who walks in the clouds" and is used to describe those who have avid imaginations and dreams, and who choose to live outside of preconceived boxes and be true to themselves. It is a combination of the words "*nephelē*" meaning "cloud" and "*batha*" which refers to a place where you can walk.

Novaturient [No-vah-ter-y-ent] – desiring or seeking powerful change in your life, behaviour or a certain situation. This word is of Latin origin and comes from the word "*novāre*" – which can be translated as "to make new." This word is primarily used to describe a compelling desire to make personal change, often relating to the desire to travel and explore different places.

Numinous [Noo-min-us] – this word describes something that seems to be filled with something divine, mighty, or deeply spiritual. It is used when something surpasses comprehension or understanding in an awe-inspiring way. It comes from the Latin word "*numen*", meaning to nod, and is derived from the idea of "the nod of the head of a divine power."

Peregrinate [peh-ree-grin-ate] – to travel and move around from one country to another, or from place to place, especially by foot. This word comes from the Latin *peregrinus* which means foreigner or travelling. The Latin word *peregrin* also means to travel abroad. The word was coined in the 16th century for use in Middle English as "peregrinate."

Resfeber [Race-fay-ber] – this word refers to the racing of a traveller's heart and the rush of emotions that they experience before embarking on a journey. This Swedish word, translated as "travel fever," describes the mixture of anxiety and expectation that often happens for travellers during this time.

Selcouth [sell-coo-th] – an English word that describes something unusual or extraordinary, or not known or experienced before – such as a new place or strange land. Derived from the Old English words "*seld*" meaning "rarely", and "*cūþ*" meaning "known"; the word "*seldcūþ*" or "selcouth" is used to describe a place that is unfamiliar or novel in some way.

Serendipity [seh-ren-dip-it-ee] – making a positive or desirable discovery by accident or chance. This word is often applied to unplanned travels in which awe-inspiring places are unexpectedly found, or when unexpected positive things happen. The origin of this word is a marvellous one – the author Horace Walpole first coined the word in 1754 when he was inspired by the Persian story of The Three Princes of Serendip.

Walpole wrote that the princes were "making discoveries by accident and sagacity of things they were not in quest of."

Smultronställe [Smoo-tron-still-eh] – a special or secret place that is close to your heart and may have sentimental or personal meaning for you. Of Swedish origin, this word literally translates as "wild strawberry patch" or "the place where wild strawberries grow." The term is used by Swedes to refer to any place off the beaten path that brings you joy.

Ukiyo [Oo-key-yoh] – this world translated literally means "the floating world." It describes living in the moment and being detached from the bothers of life, or a person who embraces life. This word is derived from an art movement that occurred between the 17th and 19th centuries in Japan in which paintings and prints depicted everyday life and simple pleasures. It has come to refer to urban lifestyle and culture, and pleasure-seeking individuals.

Waldeinsamkeit [Wild-eye-n-zam-kite] – the feeling that one may have when alone in the woods or in nature; often a spiritual or awakening experience. This is another German word, and is formed of a combination of the words "*wald*" meaning "forest" or "wild", and "*einsamkeit*" meaning "solitude". The word is best described as the positive feeling of being alone in the woods.

Wanderlust [Wun-der-luh-st] – a strong desire to travel and explore the world. We all know this one, right? This German word is an amalgamation of the words "*wandern*" meaning to hike or roam, and "*lust*" meaning pleasure or delight.

Wayfarer [Way-fair-er] – one who travels by foot. An English word that came to being as an amalgamation of the Old English words "*weg*" and "*faran*". "*Weg*" is a word that referred to a course of travel – a road, space, path, or way – in Old English. "*Faran*" meant to go, to travel, to set forth, to wander. The first known use of "wayfarer" was in the 15th Century and it was generally used to describe those journeying on foot.

Yūgen [Yoo-ghen] – a profound and deep awareness of the universe that triggers a vast emotional response and is difficult to describe. This word was first used in Chinese philosophical texts in around the year 1200 BC. It has a meaning similar to "mysterious" or "dark". The word is used widely in Japan within the arts and creative worlds. The Buddhist concept of Yūgen relates to embracing the mysterious and profound in a blend of alertness and longing.

Useful websites

Be the change you wish to see in the world. Mahatma Gandhi

Housesitting websites

House Carers
www.housecarers.com
House Carers was founded in 2000 and was one of the first websites to facilitate housesitting. It now supports sits worldwide.

House Sit Match
www.housesitmatch.com
House Sit Match was initially set up in 2014 to cover the UK and Australia, but has since expanded worldwide.

House Sitters (America, Australia, Canada, New Zealand, UK)
www.housesittersamerica.com
www.aussiehousesitters.com.au
www.housesitterscanada.com
www.kiwihousesitters.co.nz
www.housesittersuk.co.uk
Operating as different housesitting websites for each country, the "House Sitters" group are owned and operated by the same family-run business.

Mindahome
mindahome.co.uk
This website was founded in 2008 and specialises in housesits across the UK. With a filter to check whether the sitter can bring their own pets, this is the niche that helps them stand out.

Mind My House
www.mindmyhouse.com
A global housesitting website that was set up in 2005 by a couple and has expanded into a facility for more than 23,000 users.

Nomador
www.nomador.com
Launched in 2013, Nomador quickly became one of the most used Housesitting websites worldwide. Their website is user-friendly and easily enables users to search for international sitters and housesits alike.

Trusted Housesitters
www.trustedhousesitters.com
This is without doubt the "top dog" of housesitting websites, Trusted Housesitters operates in more than 130 countries worldwide and offers 24/7 free vet advice, as well as a user-friendly website and app.

Paid housesitting websites

Care.com
www.care.com/house-sitting-jobs
A website facilitating any care that is required – from child-care to senior care and, yes you guessed it, pet and house care. Selecting the pet-care option, you can find sitters and housesits across America and the UK with relative ease. The sitter approaches this as a job and charges the homeowner accordingly.

Rover.com
www.rover.com/uk
Rover operates worldwide but predominantly in the USA. It is a "pet services" business which helps pet owners find dog walkers, pet day care, drop-in visitors and housesitters. The sitters charge for their services and the homeowners book and pay via the app where they are able to view profiles and read sitters' reviews before booking.

Luxury Housesitting
www.luxuryhousesitting.com
Catering to homeowners and sitters worldwide but with the majority of housesits available in the USA and Europe. Housesitters inform homeowners of their specific fees for each housesit depending on the level of pet and house care required.

Pet first aid

Pro Training pet first aid level 2
www.protrainings.uk
A one-day fully online course in Pet First Aid which covers pet CPR, accidents, and injuries. The course will allow you to feel more confident when housesitting, make your profile stand out, and provide you with an accredited certificate.

Travel volunteering & connecting

Couchsurfing
www.couchsurfing.com
Travellers and hosts use this website to connect with each other; hosts offer free accommodation and travellers take their time to learn about local lives and the local area. The website can also be used as a platform to search for events happening worldwide.

Useful Websites

HelpX
www.helpx.net
HelpX or Help Exchange is an international online group of members consisting of volunteers and hosts. Hosts provide free accommodation and sometimes meals in exchange for time spent on a project by a volunteer. The exchange concept is broad on this website and volunteers can work anywhere from backpacker hostels to sailing boats.

Workaway
www.workaway.info
A global online community of travellers and hosts who want to see the world and give back to the places they visit. The volunteering projects range from building projects, to gardening, to childcare and the volunteer usually works/volunteers for around 25 hours per week in exchange for accommodation and meals.

Worldwide Opportunities on Organic Farms (WWOOF)
wwoof.net
WWOOF is a global movement that links travellers with organic farmers. Its aim is to provide organic farmers with help and to spread awareness and exchange knowledge of sustainable and natural farming practices – while providing travellers with accommodation, education, and cultural exchange. Founded in 1971, it was one of the world's first organisations of this type. Typically food and board are provided by hosts in exchange for volunteers' time and efforts.

Carbon calculators / offsetting schemes

Atmosfair
www.atmosfair.de/de
Atmosfair is a non-profit organisation which promotes, develops and finances renewable energies worldwide. With tools and services to assist businesses and individuals in

executing climate policies and targets, their website can be used to calculate personal or business carbon footprint as well as a search tool for legitimate carbon offsetting projects.

Gold Standard
www.goldstandard.org
Gold Standard is an organisation which manage best practice standards for offsetting projects. They have put vigorous measures in place to verify and check projects, looking closely at sustainability and environmental impacts. The Gold Standard seal is given to the most credible offsetting projects globally and is a high accolade to achieve. The projects promoted through Gold Standard also have Verified Carbon Standard (VCS) which is the world's most widely used greenhouse gas crediting initiative.

VCS Verra Registry
registry.verra.org
VCS Verra Registry is a publicly available tracker which can be used to check the generation and retirement of Verified Carbon Units (VCU's). The site has listings and information on certified projects and specific carbon units to allow full transparency and accountability checks.

Outdoor recycled gear

Patagonia
wornwear.patagonia.com
Patagonia 'Worn Wear' allows you to buy used items which are still in good condition, and if you trade in your old items they will give you credit towards your next purchase.

The North Face
www.thenorthfacerenewed.com
The North Face have an offshoot called 'North Face Renewed'; you can send in your used products and a team at

North Face inspect, repair and wash them before reselling them at a reduced price.

Vango
www.campingrecycled.co.uk
One of many outdoor companies offering used, recycled or repaired products for sale at a discount are Vango. They have set up 'Camping Recycled' whereby tents, backpacks and other outdoor adventure gear that has been used but is in good condition are resold for a discount.

Green travel choices

Booking.com Sustainability
www.sustainability.booking.com/booking-travel-sustainable
Focusing on five key areas: waste, water, support for local communities, protection of natural environments and energy and greenhouse gases, Booking.com have a "Travel Sustainable" badge which they accredit to properties that uphold these attributes. This scheme is validated by the Travalyst Independent Advisory Group.

BSpoke Tours
www.bspoketours.com
BSpoke Tours organise cycling holidays across Europe and focus on minimising the impact on the environment while maximising the adventure. New and interesting cycle routes are listed on their website along with how you can contact them for more information on trip planning.

Green Traveller
www.greentraveller.co.uk
The Green Traveller website is a good base for starting your eco-focused travel search. With tips, guides and route planning

for flight-free and eco travel, it's full of great information and will inspire you on where to go for your next low-impact holiday.

Intrepid
www.intrepidtravel.com/uk
Focusing on local communities, native wildlife, and trips with a purpose, responsible travel is at the heart of Intrepid. Operating trips worldwide, they are a B Corp accredited travel company. Visit their website to find out more about how you can make your next trip more sustainable.

Much Better Adventures
www.muchbetteradventures.com
A travel company committed to climate action through capturing twice the amount of carbon emitted by their trips, campaigning and working with local communities, Much Better Adventures are B Corp certified and focus on trips oozing with adventure. Thrill seekers – look no further for your next sustainable expedition.

Projects Abroad
www.projects-abroad.co.uk
Start your search for an ecotourism trip by looking at Projects Abroad – partners of WTM Responsible Tourism whom bring together travel companies, organisations and individuals who, through ethical practices, provide sustainable travel initiatives.

Pura Aventura
pura-aventura.com
One of the first travel companies in the UK to be certified B Corp, Pura Aventura's commitment to carbon compensation, preserving ecosystems and funding conservation projects is impressive. They concentrate on trips to a smaller number of destinations such as Costa Rica, Patagonia and the Spanish Pyrenees; adventure with a conscious.

Responsible Travel

www.responsibletravel.com

Responsible Travel has an ecotourism section specifically for you to read up on how you can contribute to the natural environment and community when you are travelling.

Green travel accreditations

Eco Tourism Australia

www.ecotourism.org.au

If you are travelling to Australia, check out this website. Eco Tourism accredits businesses that focus on sustainable resource use, tourism in natural settings and have a low impact on the environment.

European Green Capital Award

environment.ec.europa.eu/topics/urban-environment/european-green-capital-award_en

This award is given to cities in recognition of their efforts to improve the environment, economy, and quality of life for their residents. The cities awarded are leading the way in environmentally-friendly urban living and the website is a great place to look for your next city break – all previous winners are listed along with what they put in place to attain the accreditation.

Green Key England

www.greenkeyengland.co.uk

Green Key is an accolade received by tourism businesses in England such as campsites, hostels, hotels, restaurants, visitor attractions and conference centres whom can prove they adhere to green efforts under several different categories including waste, staff involvement and environmental management.

Green Tourism
www.green-tourism.com/pages/home
The Green Tourist Business scheme allows you to search for businesses in the UK – mostly hotels – to check their eco-status. They get accredited with a Green Tourism award which is graded in Gold, Silver and Bronze depending on how green they are.

Global Sustainable Tourism Council
www.gstcouncil.org
The GST Council are a body which review and regulate green initiatives put in place by several industries: accommodation, tour operators, governments, business and corporate travel companies.

Rainforest Alliance
www.rainforest-alliance.org/business/certification/how-does-the-rainforest-alliance-work-with-nepcon
The Rainforest Alliance certification means that a product has been formed by companies working together to balance manufacturing with people and nature. The alliance works with tourism businesses to educate on standards recognised by the Global Sustainable Tourism Council which they are then audited on. You can check specific hotels and businesses for the certification on their website.

Trip Advisor Green Leaders
www.tripadvisor.co.uk/GreenLeaders
Hotels and B&Bs must apply to achieve the status, given out in the form of Platinum, Gold, Silver and Bronze levels according to how green Trip Advisor deems the business. The programme was developed in consultation with the United Nations Environment Programme, Carbon Trust, UK Green Building Council and the International Tourism Partnership. Accredited accommodations have a badge on their page: a green leaf.

Modes of transport

Bla Bla Car
www.blablacar.com
A carpool and bus services app that allows users to type in where they are leaving from, and where they would like to go, and search for vehicles driving those routes that have spare seats. For a small fee toward fuel costs, you can hop in and share the trip. Primarily used within the UK and Europe.

Brittany Ferries
www.brittany-ferries.co.uk
If you are looking to travel from the UK to France or Spain, this is the website for you. With frequent services, relatively good value fares, and comfortable travel, it's never been easier to travel by sea to popular holiday spots and avoid flying.

Easyjet: Pathway to Net Zero
www.easyjet.com/en/sustainability
A great resource for reading up about how Easyjet is doing their bit for the aviation sector's carbon emissions, as well as how they have made a difference on board their flights by reducing plastic usage, investing in smarter technologies and fuels, and offsetting emissions.

National Express / Megabus / Flixbus
www.nationalexpress.com/en
www.megabus.com
www.flixbus.co.uk
Long and short distance coach travel giants, these companies can take you across the USA, Canada, UK, and the continent of Europe. With reasonably priced fares, comfortable seats, Wi-Fi, power outlets and toilets on most services, bus travel has never been so easy and relaxing.

Park4Night
park4night.com/en
With a website and app version which are both easy to navigate, this site is bursting with places you can camp or park up overnight. There are filters for free sites, paid sites and sites with certain facilities such as toilets, showers, drinking water or BBQ's. The map view is a great feature and the website shows places to stay all over the world. We've used this extensively in the UK, Australia and New Zealand.

Skyscanner Environment
www.skyscanner.net/environment
If air travel is unavoidable for you, Sky Scanner now shows you which airlines and routes are the greenest. When you've searched a route, scan the list of options and you will see a few that say something like "This flight emits 9% less CO_2." This will be based on aircraft type, capacity, stops and the directness of the route.

The Man in Seat 61
www.seat61.com
If you are planning a trip by rail anywhere in the world, Seat 61 is a great source of knowledge in this area. The website contains train times, routes, costs, and even pictures of the carriages. You can use this website to look for trains run by electricity and the best routes to take to reduce emissions.

Other useful stuff

PO Box
www.royalmail.com/receiving/po-box
For UK nationals, the link above will take you to the Royal Mail website where you can set up a PO box for a fee; meaning you can collect it from the PO box when you are back in the country. This is a great option if you are on the road for long periods of time and have no home address.

Useful Websites

Recycling clothing
www.recyclenow.com/recycle-an-item/clothing-textiles
A great resource for people living or travelling in the UK; this website tells you where your nearest recycling centres are – including those which accept clothing and textiles – and can help you to arrange a collection from your home address if you need.

Bibliography

Abookire, Susan. "Can forest therapy enhance health and well-being?". *Harvard Medical School: Exercise and fitness.* 29 May, 2020. https://www.health.harvard.edu/blog/can-forest-therapy-enhance-health-and-well-being-2020052919948

"Addressing climate change". *American Airlines.* https://news.aa.com/esg/climate-change/ (accessed March 27, 2023)

"Average weekly household expenditure on cleaning materials in the United Kingdom (UK) in 2021, by age of household reference person," in section: Furniture, Furnishings and Household items. *Statista.* 27 July 2022. https://www.statista.com/statistics/285609/cleaning-products-weekly-uk-household-expenditure-by-age/ (accessed November 8, 2022)

Biddle, Pippa. *Ours to Explore: Privilege, Power and the Paradox of Voluntourism.* Potomac Books, 2021.

"Calculate your carbon footprint: How to Help." *The Nature Conservancy.* https://www.nature.org/en-us/get-involved/how-to-help/carbon-footprint-calculator/#:~:text=A%20carbon%20footprint%20is%20the,is%20closer%20to%204%20tons (accessed November 29, 2022)

Cleveland Heartlab. "Do pets help your heart?". *ClevelandHeartLab.* 09 March, 2020. https://www.clevelandheartlab.com/blog/do-pets-help-your-heart/ (accessed April 3, 2023)

Coffey, Helen. *Zero Altitude: How I learned to fly less and travel more.* Flint, 2022.

"Costa Rica: the 'living Eden' designing a template for a cleaner, carbon-free world." *United Nations Environment Programme.* https://www.unep.org/news-and-stories/story/costa-rica-living-eden-

Bibliography

designing-template-cleaner-carbon-free-world (accessed November 21, 2022)

Cox, Lisa., and Morton, Adam. "'Devastating': 91% of reefs surveyed on Great Barrier Reef affected by coral bleaching in 2022". *The Guardian.* 10 May, 2022. https://www.theguardian.com/environment/2022/may/10/devastating-90-of-reefs-surveyed-on-great-barrier-reef-affected-by-coral-bleaching-in-2022 (accessed October 12, 2022)

Crippa, M., Guizzardi, D., Muntean, M., Schaaf, E., Solazzo, E., Monforti-Ferrario, F., Olivier, J.G.J., Vignati, E. "Fossil CO2 emissions of all world countries – 2020 Report". *European Commission.* 09 September, 2020. https://publications.jrc.ec.europa.eu/repository/handle/JRC121460 (accessed October 13, 2022)

Csáky, Corinna. "Keeping Children Out of Harmful Institutions". *Save the Children.* 2009. https://www.coe.int/t/dg3/children/childrenincare/Keeping%20Children%20Out%20of%20Harmful%20Institutions%20Final%2020.11.09.pdf (accessed March 2, 2023)

Daley-Olmert, Meg. "DOG GOOD: The latest on the biology of the human-animal bond." *Psychology Today.* 05 May, 2010. https://www.psychologytoday.com/intl/blog/made-each-other/201005/dog-good (accessed April 3, 2023)

Dickinson, Joanna. "What is Slow Tourism? The next big hospitality trend". *EHL insights.* https://hospitalityinsights.ehl.edu/what-slow-tourism (accessed December 4, 2022)

"Dose of nature is just what the doctor ordered". *The University of Queensland, Australia.* 24 June 2016. https://www.uq.edu.au/news/article/2016/06/dose-of-nature-is-just-what-doctor-ordered#:~:text=People%20who%20visit%20parks%20for%2030%20minutes%20or,new%20research%20by%20Australian%20and%20UK%20environmental%20scientists (accessed April 3, 2023)

Dottle, Rachael., and Gu, Jackie. "The U.S. throws away up to 11.3 million tons of textile waste each year—around 2,150 pieces of clothing each second." *Bloomberg.* https://www.bloomberg.com/graphics/2022-fashion-industry-environmental-impact/ (accessed November 19, 2022)

Durr, James. "Top 10 Eco Tourist Hotels Across the UK". *Ecobnb.* 22 November, 2021. https://ecobnb.com/blog/2021/11/eco-tourist-hotels-across-uk/ (accessed October 30, 2022)

"Eco retreats: Best places to Stay in Eco-retreats". *Cool Places.* https://www.coolplaces.co.uk/places-to-stay/eco-retreats (accessed November 2, 2022)

Edwards, Karen. *The Responsible Traveller.* Summersdale, 2022.

Fitzgerald, Sunny. "The secret to mindful travel? A walk in the woods". *National Geographic Travel.* 18 October, 2019. https://www.nationalgeographic.com/travel/article/forest-bathing-nature-walk-health (accessed April 5, 2023)

"Fuel efficiency and emissions reduction". *United Airlines.* https://www.united.com/ual/en/us/fly/company/global-citizenship/environment/fuel-efficiency-and-emissions-reduction.html (accessed December 11, 2022)

Hammond, Richard. *The Green Traveller: Conscious adventure that doesn't cost the earth.* Pavilion Books, 2023.

Haslam, Chris., Claire Irvin, Cathy Adams and Ann Morgan. "The Times and The Sunday Times Travel Team." Talk at the *Cheltenham Literature Festival*, Cheltenham Town Hall. Oct 12 2022.

Honey, Martha., and Frenkiel, Kelsey. *Overtourism: Lessons for a better future.* Island Press, 2021.

Hughes, Lauren. "Benefits of cold water swimming explained by health experts". *Woman and Home: Health and Wellbeing.* 18 January, 2023. https://www.womanandhome.com/health-wellbeing/benefits-of-wild-swimming/ (accessed April 6, 2023)

"Israel's housing policies in occupied Palestinian territory amount to racial segregation – UN experts," press release from, *United Nations.* https://www.ohchr.org/en/press-releases/2022/04/israels-housing-policies-occupied-palestinian-territory-amount-racial (accessed December 13, 2022)

Jepsen Trangsrud, LK., Borg, M., Bratland-Sanda, S., Klevan, T. "Embodying Experiences with Nature in Everyday Life Recovery for Persons with Eating Disorders". *International Journal of Environmental Research and Public Health.* 17(8), 2784. 17 April, 2020. https://www.mdpi.com/1660-4601/17/8/2784/htm (accessed April 2, 2023)

Jervis, Nina. "Top Eco-Friendly & Sustainable Retreats in the UK and Worldwide". *Host Unusual.* 07 March, 2022. https://hostunusual.com/news/view-all/top-eco-friendly-sustainable-retreats-in-the-uk-and-worldwide/ (accessed October 30, 2022)

Karnikowski, Nina. *Go Lightly: How to travel without hurting the planet.* Laurence King Publishing, 2021.

Bibliography

Kayser, Beth. "What is the average carbon footprint, globally?" *Pawprint eco companion.* https://www.pawprint.eco/eco-blog/average-carbon-footprint-globally (accessed October 13, 2022)

Kinsman, Juliet. *Travel: The Green Edit.* Ebury Press, 2021.

Kommenda, Niko. "How your flight emits as much CO2 as many people do in a year." *The Guardian.* 19 July, 2019. https://www.theguardian.com/environment/ng-interactive/2019/jul/19/carbon-calculator-how-taking-one-flight-emits-as-much-as-many-people-do-in-a-year (accessed October 5, 2022)

Kotera, Yasuhiro., Richardson, Miles., and Sheffield, David. "Effects of Shinrin-Yoku (Forest Bathing) and Nature Therapy on Mental Health: a Systematic Review and Meta-analysis." *International Journal of Mental Health and Addiction 20.* 337–361 (2022). https://link.springer.com/article/10.1007/s11469-020-00363-4 (accessed April 3, 2023)

Lepere, Imogen. *The Ethical Traveller.* Smith Street Books, 2022.

Li, Ketong. "High on Helping: The Dangers of Voluntourism". *The New York Times.* 17 June, 2022. https://www.nytimes.com/2022/06/17/learning/high-on-helping-the-dangers-of-voluntourism.html (accessed March 3, 2023)

Li, Qing. "Effects of forest bathing (shinrin-yoku) on serotonin in serum, depressive symptoms and subjective sleep quality in middle-aged males". *Nippon Medical School.* November, 2022. https://www.researchgate.net/profile/Qing-Li-88 (accessed April 5, 2023)

Lonely Planet. *Sustainable Escapes.* Lonely Planet, 2020.

Lonely Planet. *The Digital Nomad Handbook.* Lonely Planet, 2020.

Lonely Planet. *The Sustainable Travel Handbook.* Lonely Planet, 2020.

Louv, Richard. *Last Child in the Woods: Saving Our Children from Nature-Deficit Disorder.* Atlantic Books, 2010.

Martin, Laura. "The Best Eco-Retreats in the UK". *Esquire.* 20 April, 2021. https://www.esquire.com/uk/design/a36096853/best-eco-retreats-uk/ (accessed November 2, 2022)

Matonti, T., Gitto , P. ., and McGrann, K. "The Effects of Equine Therapy on Military Veterans with PTSD." *Journal of Student Research, 10*(4), November, 2021. https://www.jsr.org/hs/index.php/path/article/view/2001#:~:text=Initi

al%20results%20showed%20decreased%20anxiety,for%20veterans%20suffering%20from%20PTSD (accessed April 4, 2023)

"Nature and Mental Health." *Mind*. November, 2021. https://www.mind.org.uk/information-support/tips-for-everyday-living/nature-and-mental-health/how-nature-benefits-mental-health/ (accessed April 2, 2023)

Nett, Stephen. "The Healing Powers of Nature". *Sonoma County Regional Parks*. March, 2018. https://parks.sonomacounty.ca.gov/learn/blog/park-blogs/the-healing-powers-of-nature#:~:text=One%20of%20the%20first%20clinical,view%20of%20a%20brick%20wall (accessed April 3, 2023)

"Net-Zero by 2050." *Easyjet*. https://www.easyjet.com/en/sustainability#:~:text=Our%20pathway%20to%20Net%20Zero,zero%20carbon%20emissions%20by%202050 (accessed January 27, 2023)

"New plans unveiled to boost recycling," press release from, *Department for Environment, Food and Rural Affairs. UK Government*. 07 May, 2021. https://www.gov.uk/government/news/new-plans-unveiled-to-boost-recycling#:~:text=Under%20proposals%20unveiled%20by%20ministers,that%20attracts%20flies%20and%20pests. (accessed November 7, 2022)

Petch, Danielle. "Your member code of conduct". *Trusted Housesitters*. 10 September, 2021. https://www.trustedhousesitters.com/blog/news/code-of-conduct/ (accessed December 10, 2022)

Peters, Steve. *The Chimp Paradox: The Mind Management Programme for Confidence, Success and Happiness*. Vermilion, 2012.

Qureshi, AI., Memon, MZ., Vazquez, G., and Suri, MF. "Cat ownership and the Risk of Fatal Cardiovascular Diseases. Results from the Second National Health and Nutrition Examination Study Mortality Follow-up Study." *Journal of Vascular and Interventional Neurology*. 2009 2(1), 132-5. https://www.ncbi.nlm.nih.gov/pmc/articles/PMC3317329/ (accessed April 4, 2023)

Rhodes, Christine. "The healing power of pets". *Healthcare Counselling and Psychotherapy Journal*. October, 2020. https://www.bacp.co.uk/bacp-journals/healthcare-counselling-and-psychotherapy-journal/october-2020/the-healing-power-of-pets/#:~:text=Animals%20have%20the%20ability%20to,supported%20by%20the%20oxytocin%20hypothesis.&text=The%20hypothesis%20suggests%20that%2C%20in,bonding%20and%20increased%20prosocial%20behaviour (accessed April 3, 2023)

Bibliography

Ritchie, Hannah., Roser, Max., and Rosado, Pablo. "CO_2 and greenhouse gas emissions". *Our world in data.* https://ourworldindata.org/co2-emissions (accessed October 12, 2022)

Robbins, Jim. "Ecopsychology: How Immersion in Nature Benefits Your Health". *Yale School of the Environment.* 14 July, 2016. https://e360.yale.edu/features/ecopsychology-how-immersion-in-nature-benefits-your-health (accessed April 3, 2023)

Rosenberg, Tina. "The business of voluntourism: do western do-gooders actually do harm?" *The Guardian.* 13 September, 2018. https://www.theguardian.com/news/2018/sep/13/the-business-of-voluntourism-do-western-do-gooders-actually-do-harm (accessed March 3, 2023)

Sifferlin, Alexandra. "The healing power of nature". *Time.* 14 July, 2016. https://time.com/4405827/the-healing-power-of-nature/ (accessed April 2, 2023)

Smith, Phoebe. "Thailand cove made famous in The Beach reopens to visitors after four-year closure". *The Guardian.* 16 May 2022. https://www.theguardian.com/travel/2022/may/16/thailand-cove-made-famous-in-the-beach-reopens-to-visitors-after-four-year-closure (accessed October 12, 2022)

Srámek P, Simecková M, Janský L, Savlíková J, Vybíral S. "Human physiological responses to immersion into water of different temperatures." *European Journal of Applied Physiology.* 81(5). March, 2000, 436-42.

"Sustainable Red Sea Diving and Eco-Initiatives." *Ecotourism World.* 20 May, 2022. https://ecotourism-world.com/sustainable-red-sea-diving-and-eco-initiatives/ (accessed October 10, 2022)

Taranath, Anu. *Beyond Guilt Trips: Mindful Travel in an Unequal World.* Between the Lines, 2019.

"10 of the best eco hotels in the UK". *The Independent.* 08 October, 2021. https://www.independent.co.uk/climate-change/sustainable-living/uk-eco-hotels-sustainability-best-b1931885.html (accessed November 3, 2022)

"The healing power of animals: benefits of animal-assisted therapy". Blog, *Husson University.* 20 July, 2022. https://www.husson.edu/online/blog/2022/07/benefits-of-animal-assisted-therapy (accessed April 2, 2023)

Thiessen, Tamara. "Australia Bushfires Burn Tourism Industry: $4.5 Billion As Holidayers Cancel". *Forbes.* 20 January 2020.

https://www.forbes.com/sites/tamarathiessen/2020/01/20/australia-bushfires-hit-tourism-industry-as-holidayers-cancel/?sh=6d579a6d72c5 (accessed October 19, 2022)

Tuppen, Holley. *Sustainable Travel: The essential guide to positive impact adventures.* 2021, White Lion Publishing.

"2020 UK Greenhouse Gas Emissions, Final Figures." *Department for Business, Energy and Industrial Strategy.* National Statistics. 01 February, 2022. https://assets.publishing.service.gov.uk/government/uploads/system/uploads/attachment_data/file/1051408/2020-final-greenhouse-gas-emissions-statistical-release.pdf (accessed November 9, 2022)

Watson, Penny. *Slow Travel: Reconnecting with the world at your own pace.* Hardie Grant, 2019.

Woodley, Danny. "How Much Does it Cost to Kennel a Dog or Cat in the UK in 2022?". *Job prices.* https://job-prices.co.uk/kennel-costs/#:~:text=Cats,we%20last%20checked%20the%20prices (accessed November 17, 2022)

Zaiontz, Cody. "The healing power of animals". *Psychiatric Times.* https://www.psychiatrictimes.com/view/the-healing-power-of-animals (accessed April 3, 2023.

Author Bio

Jessica Holmes grew up in Gloucester, U.K., and has always felt a deep connection for nature and animals. Her passion for travel encouraged her to give up her dream job as a police investigator and backpack her way around the world. She has lived nomadically for long periods of her adult life. Struggling with the inevitable environmental impact of a high-intensity travel lifestyle, she sought a new path which could revolutionise modern travel. She now housesits full time around the world.

Website: www.hitchedandhiking.com

Instagram: @hitchedhikingandhousesitting

Milton Keynes UK
Ingram Content Group UK Ltd.
UKHW020820231023
431156UK00011B/126

9 781914 390173